More Praise for *Chief Customer Officer 2.0*

"Jeanne focused our leadership team on embedding her five competencies into how we do business. Using the content described here, she united us in redirecting how we develop and grow our business and customer relationships."

—Doug Holte, President, Irvine Company Office Properties

"I *guarantee* that you will dog-ear this book and refer to it repeatedly to achieve success in your customer experience transformation and leadership role."

—Gavan Duff, Chief Customer Officer, MSA,
The Safety Company

"It's wonderful to see Jeanne Bliss come out with another great book. Chief Customer Officer 2.0 is full of sound, practical advice for leaders who want to help their organizations become more customer-centric. I highly recommend it for anyone who cares about customer experience."

—Bruce Temkin, Managing Partner of Temkin Group,
Co-Founder, Customer Experience Professionals Association

"Jeanne Bliss was the first to bring the chief customer officer role and customer leadership to us. With this book she continues to be a guardian and beacon to customer experience executives around the world."

—Kerry Bodine, Coauthor of *Outside In: The Power of Putting*
Customers at the Center of Your Business

"Jeanne's five competencies in this book gave us a clear and concise path for improving client experiences and uniting our leadership team."

—Dan Schrider, CEO, Sandy Spring Bank

"If you believe, like I do, that companies in today's increasingly commoditized world need to be customer-driven and experience-focused, then grab Jeanne Bliss's *Chief Customer Officer 2.0* off the shelf, read, and absorb it. Create such a position dedicated to developing a growth engine around the individual, living, breathing customers of your company, fulfill that position, or align with that person. Or, you know, be commoditized."

—Joe Pine, Coauthor, *The Experience Economy* and
Infinite Possibility

"This is simply the most important book on your reading list right now to help you drive your customer experience transformation."

—**Joe Wheeler, Executive Director, The Service Profit Chain Institute**

There is no one more qualified to write this book than Jeanne Bliss, a visionary and leading light in the search for what customer-centric leaders must do to propel their organizations to greater success. Read *Chief Customer Officer 2.0* to capitalize on Jeanne's decades of experience as a practitioner and coach, and learn how to truly embed customer-centric competencies into your organization.

—**Bob Thompson, CEO of CustomerThink Corp. and author of *Hooked On Customers: The Five Habits of Legendary Customer-Centric Companies***

"Make this book first on your reading list! Jeanne Bliss's thought leadership and ability to unite a leadership team and clarify this work takes years off your customer experience transformation."

—**Yves Leduc, President, Velan, Inc.**

"No matter your role in business, run to the cash register with this book. In *Chief Customer Officer 2.0*, you are provided a model, set of filters, tangible game plan, and the tools you will need to enjoy rewarding and sustainable growth that comes from delighting your customers. The book you are holding is approachable, transformational, and in keeping with the incredible thought leadership Jeanne Bliss has offered throughout her customer-obsessed career!"

—**Joseph Michelli, *New York Times* bestselling author of *Leading the Starbucks Way*, *The Zappos Experience*, and *The New Gold Standard***

This book should be a reality show because almost every company needs a makeover to make customers a priority again. *Chief Customer Officer 2.0* is the best guide for your own successful makeover!

—**Jeffrey Hayzlett, primetime TV and radio host, speaker, author, and part-time cowboy**

"Jeanne Bliss has the experience and wisdom to guide you through the process of creating a customer-driven organization."

—**Shep Hyken, customer service expert and *New York Times* bestselling author of *The Amazement Revolution***

Chief Customer Officer 2.0

Chief Customer Officer 2.0

How to Build Your Customer-Driven Growth Engine

(Completely Revised and Expanded)

Jeanne Bliss

JB JOSSEY-BASS
A Wiley Imprint
www.josseybass.com

Published by John Wiley & Sons, Inc., Hoboken, New Jersey.
Published simultaneously in Canada.

For general information on our other products and services or for technical support, please contact our Customer Care Department within the United States at (800) 762-2974, outside the United States at (317) 572-3993 or fax (317) 572-4002.

Wiley publishes in a variety of print and electronic formats and by print-on-demand. Some material included with standard print versions of this book may not be included in e-books or in print-on-demand. If this book refers to media such as a CD or DVD that is not included in the version you purchased, you may download this material at http://booksupport.wiley.com. For more information about Wiley products, visit www.wiley.com.

Library of Congress Cataloging-in-Publication Data:

ISBN 9781119047605 (Hardcover)
ISBN 9781119047629 (ePDF)
ISBN 9781119047643 (ePub)

Cover design: Wiley

Printed in the United States of America

10 9 8 7 6 5 4 3 2

For All the Leaders Who Grow Their Businesses
by Improving Customers' Lives

Contents

Introduction

I've been doing this work for so long, that sometimes while I'm waxing on, a Chief Customer Officer (CCO) client will ask, "Can you write that down?" I don't often do that, because my goal in coaching CCOs and leadership teams is for them to find their own united voice. To help them emerge as customer leaders. We unite the CCO and executive team in focusing their organizations on customer-driven growth. On replacing reactivity and survey score addiction with embedded competencies that became part of the business engine. My job is behind the scenes to ensure they don't fall into the same potholes others before them have, and to help them accelerate their transformation as swiftly as possible.

In the past ten 10 years, since writing and publishing *Chief Customer Officer: Getting Past Lip Service to Passionate Action*, it has been my privilege to be called upon by nearly every business vertical around the world—to coach their Chief Customer Officer and executive leadership teams in their transformation toward customer-driven growth. Insurance, technology, healthcare, retail, financial services, hospitality, manufacturing, telecommunications, Software-as-Service companies, service businesses, government agencies, and many other industry leaders have reached out for clarity and a road map on how to navigate these often-unwieldy waters. *(Usually starting with a somewhat urgent call asking for help defining the work and the role. You are not alone!)* Like you, they needed a way to break this work up and accomplish it in a realistic manner.

We have made great strides together. And we have stories to tell. These stories from both clients and customer leadership executives representing nearly every business vertical are peppered throughout this book in case studies entitled "My Rock, My Story." This title is a nod to Sisyphus, who we all at times feel akin to, pushing the rock up the hill.

And that is why I have written this book for you. I wanted to provide this advanced toolkit as your success accelerator and road map. To that end, this is essentially a completely new book with specific tales of customization and implementation comprised from working with practitioners in multiple industries, organizations, and cultures.

Through working with leaders around the world, heightened specifics and tactics have emerged to increase success for this role and customer-centric business transformations. Through coaching, more tools have been established to provide greater clarity for CEOs and executive teams seeking to understand the value in this role and their personal commitment required to make it a success. Through coaching, five Customer Leadership Competencies have emerged that create an engine for reliably leading this work.

Around the world, the customer leadership executive role (chief customer officer, vice president of customer experience, etc.) has been embraced in both business-to-business and business-to-consumer organizations. Leaders in these roles have worked to figure out how they should organize, act, and make decisions to earn the right to business growth by embracing employees and customers and delivering an experience they want to have again and tell others about. There have been many versions of success, as you probably know well from living within the constraints of trying to do this work across a silo-driven organization. And many opportunities remain—through learning from each other and sharing our stories.

Helping you achieve success as CCO with your executive team and organization depends upon actions and behaviors that have been developed, practiced, and matured through my many years as a practitioner and coach. I will share these with you.

- The common denominators to customer leadership executive success.
- Roadblocks for organizations that were stopped short.
- Five Customer Leadership Competencies of world-class companies.
- What changes when the five competencies become a part of the way you go to market, develop products, reward people, and conduct annual planning.

Many things have *not* changed since I wrote *Chief Customer Officer: Getting Past Lip Service to Passionate Action*. Organizations still rely primarily on areas of expertise or silos to run the business. Annual planning is still done (mostly) silo by silo. Lagging indicator surveys still often drive point-in-time action to try to improve results (not always the customer experience) and the customer is often still the only one experiencing the outcome of this disconnection.

What *has* changed is the power that social media has given customers to speak out about their experiences. I am supremely enthused about this forcing function! Lagging survey metrics can't catch surges of happiness and unhappiness that customers express in social media to make an impact on customer growth and profitability. And the cherry-picked silo-based projects that emerge from these results are not solving the problems causing customers to depart or grow.

The monthly CEO report out still goes from silo vice president to silo vice president in C-Suite meetings. But there is growing angst that this dissected view is not the right one to make focused and impactful customer growth investments.

And with that, more companies are trying to figure out how to organize and unite to tackle experiences end to end. It's a noble commitment... but still misunderstood. Now more than ever with the rise of social media, big data, and the surge of focus on customer experience, CCOs are at risk of chasing the 'shiny object' of the moment than at embedding a set of behaviors that will transform their organizations.

So with all of that in mind, here is the inside of my new and improved clock on how to become what I call "the human duct tape" of the organization. *Chief Customer Officer 2.0* is for you, the …

- Customer leadership executives with the role today
- CEOs and boards considering the role for their organization
- Those moving to CCO from another role
- People aspiring to bring the role into their organization
- Executive Teams working with the CCO
- Recruiters placing customer leadership executive positions

Thanks for all the years of reaching out and trusting me to help you along the way. I wrote this for you, as always, to have my hand on the small of your back, encouraging and prodding you to push that rock up that hill. I am honored we get to spend this time together again. Supporting you is my life's work. Thanks for taking the time to read this new and enriched material.

Jeanne Bliss
Los Angeles, California
February 2015

Your Reading Road Map for *Chief Customer Officer 2.0*

Having prescribed to all my clients that they need to give employees and customers a road map on the experience that they deliver, the following is your reading road map for Chief Customer Officer 2.0. This book is assembled to enable you to work with your leadership team to establish a one-company approach and understanding of what it means to focus on "customer experience." It will provide you with a framework that can be customized to your organization so that you can earn the right to customer-driven growth. Through the "Action Lab" tools and "My Rock, My Story" case studies, it will challenge you to determine how your current efforts compare to others doing the same, it will provide encouragement in storytelling, and it will provide practical actions you can implement.

Chapter	Purpose
1. Chief Customer Officer Role Clarity	Summary of the CCO role based on the five-customer leadership competencies.
2. Unite Leadership to Ensure Role Adoption and Acceleration	How to lay the groundwork for a successful transformation.
3. Competency 1: Honor and Manage Customers as Assets 4. Competency 2: Align around Experience 5. Competency 3: Build a Customer Listening Path 6. Competency 4: Proactive Experience Reliability and Innovation 7. Competency 5: Leadership, Accountability, and Culture	Information on each competency to customize and implement actions for your organization.
8. Staging the Work	Maturity Map so you can stage the work and the evolution of the CCO role for your business.
9. Comprehensive Toolkit for Hiring or Interviewing a CCO. There is valuable information here for • CCO candidates • Executives and Boards considering the role • Headhunters recruiting for the role	Prepares you for the successful research and selection of a customer leadership executive for your organization.

Chief Customer Officer Role Clarity

A Chief Customer Officer is successful when he or she can simplify how the organization works together to achieve customer-driven growth, engage the leadership team, and connect the work to a return on investment. That's what everyone wants to know about this role. What does the Chief Customer Officer do, how is the work staged and what is its impact? You'll find the answers to these questions in this book.

What you will also find, which is equally important, is how to unite the leadership team and organization to 'earn the right' to growth by making decisions and orienting business operations to improve customers' lives. This is the elusive and challenging element of this work that, when neglected, can turn it into a program or project rather than a transformation. Sustainable change will occur only when this work goes beyond project plans and status updates and is grounded in caring about customers' lives. It's the path to growth the five competencies outlined in this book provides.

What I know from over thirty years as a CCO practitioner and coach to customer leadership executives and their C-Suite, is that we've got to take the reactive nature out of this work. Our work must be about embedding behaviors and competencies in the organization: Competencies that will transform how the business and operation are run, to achieve customer-driven growth.

If you became the customer "Velcro man" or "Velcro woman" where all customer issues were strewn in your path upon assuming this role, you know that establishing role clarity and executive alignment is paramount. Without it, you run the risk of being defined as the fix-it person. And that's *not* who you want to be.

Customer-focused efforts are often highly reactive because they sync to the cycle of survey results. The results come out; the silos react independently, rinse and repeat. This reactive nature of waiting for the results and then taking actions that chase the score push the work to what I call "whack-a mole" tactics. Fixing things. Project plans or work streams with red, yellow, and green dots.

And the role of the chief customer officer (CCO) is defined as the fix-it person for what currently ails customers, or the one nagging the silos to take action. Despite all this activity (giving a false positive of commitment measured by energy expended), we have not embedded new behaviors for how we understand customers' lives, how we care about their lives, and how we improve their lives. **Our work is defined by project plan movement rather than customer life improvement.**

The purpose of our work is to galvanize the organization to deliver experiences that customers want to have again—to earn the right to customer-driven growth. But what we sometimes do in these roles is the opposite. Customer-focused actions are one-off reactions to survey results, or to an executive in the field getting direct customer feedback, or to a letter that lands on someone's desk. Information is delivered, the silos react, and the cycle repeats.

As a result, the higher purpose of our work, which is to drive growth, is lost. These efforts then fall prey to being perceived as costs without reward. CEOs and boards *want* to be customer focused, but without an explicit connection to growth, many consider the work to be:

- A leap of faith.
- Expensive.
- Deterrents to the "real" work.

The Five Customer Leadership Competencies

For customer experience efforts to become valued and considered critical to driving growth they must rise above the fray of being defined as problem solving or chasing survey scores. The work must be defined as building your customer-driven growth engine, with the CCO role as the architect of that engine.

From being a practitioner in the rinse and repeat cycle to coaching CCOs and the C-Suite, I knew I had to find a way to break that cycle. To create a system that shows a clear and simple connection to a return on investment, and gives the CEO that legacy that he or she wants to leave as their mark. That system is these five competencies that will, over time, build your customer-driven growth engine.

The 5 Customer Leadership Competencies connect to growth. They deliver constantly updated information to unite leaders on the most impactful customer priorities, and they shift attitudes from chasing survey scores to caring about and improving customer lives to earn the right to growth.

Here are the benefits of this five-competency business engine:

- They establish the connection to business growth. The five competencies elevate customer experience efforts from getting a score to 'earning the right' to growth.

- You build them *at your own pace*, with actions that are most potent for your culture, your leaders, and the company's ability to take on the work within each competency.
- They build an engine analogous to the familiar process of product development, with distinguishable steps and metrics and performance requirements. These five competencies provide an equal discipline for focused customer experience development.
- They drive a one-company focus on customer experiences by uniting leaders in investing in the most impactful priorities. Competency five, for example, builds a monthly process (called a customer room) to step people into the shoes of the customer, uniting the company to focus on a few critical actions rather than having every silo choosing many tactics separately from one another.
- They specify actions that demystify the role of the customer leadership executive (CCO, CXO, etc.). The role becomes clear, as architect and facilitator of the engine, uniting leaders to make decisions that improve customers' lives and lead to business growth.

I call these <u>Customer Leadership Competencies</u> because they define the behavior of world-class organizations focused on customers and employees. They impact how these organizations decide to grow, how they lead in unison, how they identify and resolve issues, and how they collectively build a one-company experience.

Below is an introduction of the five competencies that will comprise your customer-driven growth engine. Later in the book there is a full chapter on each competency, along with tools to help you to customize your version of these competencies for your organization. These are:

- **Action Lab:** Tools and templates to immediately put into use.
- **My Rock, My Story:** CCO stories on how they united leadership, worked through challenges, and achieved success.

Based on working as a practitioner, and with clients around the globe for over thirty years, here is the *real-world* approach for how to integrate the discipline and role of customer experience leadership into your operation. **Here are the five competencies that define the Chief Customer Officer role** and require engagement of the executive team and organization to make them a success.

1: HONOR AND MANAGE CUSTOMERS AS ASSETS.

Know the Growth and Loss of Customers and Care About 'WHY?'

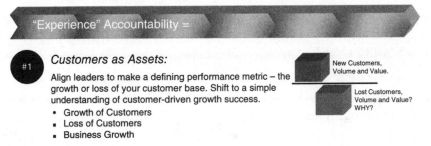

"Experience" Accountability =

#1 — *Customers as Assets:*
Align leaders to make a defining performance metric – the growth or loss of your customer base. Shift to a simple understanding of customer-driven growth success.
- Growth of Customers
- Loss of Customers
- Business Growth

New Customers, Volume and Value.

Lost Customers, Volume and Value? WHY?

In Competency 1, the work is to align leaders to make a defining performance metric—the growth or loss of the customer base. The purpose is to shift to a simple understanding of the overall success achieved when a company earns customer-driven growth.

Customer Asset Management is to know *what customers actually did* to impact business growth or loss versus what they *say they might do* via survey results.

For example: how many new customers did you bring in this quarter, by volume and value (power of your acquisition engine); how many customers were lost this quarter, by volume and value (power of the experience and value perceived); how many increased their purchases; and how many reduced their level of engagement with you? The key here is to express these outcomes in whole numbers, not retention rates, so the full impact is understood—these numbers represent the lives of customers joining or leaving your company.

This connection can be explained and accepted by your board of directors. And it gives your executives a platform from which they can personally talk about this work, take ownership of it, and connect it to business growth.

The role of the CCO is not to build and then 'pitch' these metrics to the C-Suite. It is to unite leaders in establishing customer asset metrics and customer growth behaviors that they will stand behind as a united leadership team. And it is to work to build the engine with them to enable the data so that this information is recurring and refreshed to drive business decisions.

What this means is to know and care about, at the executive level, the shifting behavior within your customer base that indicates if their bond with you is growing or shrinking. And, importantly, it's about engaging your executives in caring about the "WHY?" Why did customers stay or leave, buy more or less, or actively use your products or services more or less?

With this book, you'll be able to start the conversation with your leadership team and engage them in building your version of customer asset metrics. You will be able to engage them in building your company's version of this simple metric, and translating and communicating it across your organization, in a manner that connects to your operation and resonates with your employees.

Elevating Our Donors as Assets

Martin Hand
Chief Donor/Customer Officer
St. Jude Children's Research Hospital

Martin Hand is Chief Donor/Customer Officer at St. Jude Children's Research Hospital, where he is responsible for the overall donor experience, contact center operations, and donor account processing functions. Martin was previously Senior Vice President of Customer Experience at United Continental Holdings.

It takes $2 million per day to operate St. Jude Children's Research Hospital to help save children's lives. Donors caring about these kids have contributed over 75 percent of those funds for more than 50 years. Without them we couldn't have pushed the overall childhood cancer survival rate from 20 percent to 80 percent. Therefore we want to connect all of our employees to the importance of how their work impacts donors' lives, and to find effective and simple ways to measure and discuss the growth or shrinkage of our donor base. Our goal is to elevate this donor-centric philosophy across the organization and make the donor experience a key part of how we measure our success.

What we find is that it is most powerful to combine story telling when we deliver this information. We will tell the growth of donors and how many we did not keep, and then we will challenge the organization with the impact of losing donors. We tell this story in both the number of lost donors and also in the value of the donor we lost—to show the potential future revenue of a lost donor.

We show explicitly the incremental growth that we would have if we kept 5 or 10 or 20 percent more donors. And then we attach that information to examples of issues that drive donors away. Now people's work is connected to growth and they have clarity about what they can do about it.

2: ALIGN AROUND EXPERIENCE.

Give Leaders a Framework for Guiding the Work of the Organization.
Unite Accountability as Customers Experience You. Not Down Your Silos.

"Experience" Accountability =

Awareness & Research	Assess & Sample	Develop Solution	Partner & Contract	Service & Support	Strategic Partnership

Align Around Experience:
Align the Operation Around Customer Experience Delivery & Innovation. "Earn the Right" to Customer Asset Growth.
- Customer Journey
- Focus on Priorities
- Leadership Language

Competency 2 gives leaders a framework for guiding the work of the organization: requiring cross-silo accountability to deliver deliberate customer experiences. It unites the organization in building a framework for 'earning the right' to customer asset growth. The role of the CCO is to unite leaders and the organization in building a one-company version of their customer journey.

This means facilitating across the silos to unite them in the development, and understanding of the entire customer journey, versus the silo-based processes that dictate the customer experience (such as the sales process, marketing acquisition process, etc.). It includes focusing the organization on priority one-company experiences. And on changing the conversations from silo-driven conversations to collaborative conversations about customers' lives—their experiences across the journey they have with your organization. Over time, this will evolve leadership language to drive performance along the customer journey, driving accountability to journey stages, not only down silos.

As a result of competency two, questions about silo and project performance will shift to include accountability for customer life improvement. Your customer journey framework will provide a disciplined one-company diagnosis into the reasons behind customer asset growth or loss. And it will establish rigor in understanding and caring about priorities in customers' lives (The *real* power in journey mapping.)

With this book, you will be able to assess how you currently use your customer journey map as the framework to consistently drive company focus, in your customer listening, experience improvement, and planning efforts. You will learn how other CCOs have avoided the "shiny object" syndrome that journey-mapping is at risk of being today. And you will learn how to move mapping from a one-off activity to the beginning of a competency that drives business behavior.

How We Built Our Customer Eco-System

Lesley Mottla
Senior Vice President, Customer Experience at LAUNCH
Previously EVP, Global Product & Customer Experience, Zipcar

Lesley Mottla was part of the management team that developed Zipcar's award-winning customer experience and technologies. She just joined LAUNCH, a start-up devoted to reinventing multichannel consumer experiences.

To get started with customer experience, we built a very simple high-level customer journey on one page so everyone could understand it.

We call it our eco-system. Here's what's included: At the top are the activities and moments of truth customers go through, in the middle they are bucketed into high-level touchpoints, or stages as some call them. These are what we call "front of the house"—what customers see. Then below the stages are the "back of house" items—the things we have to unite on to deliver seamlessly to the front of the house. Presenting the visual on one page was very important for us in communications and creating understanding.

To build this map we started internally with our people, then we did a lot of observations with customers to build out the specific front-of-house components. When we started working on the micro-processes under these, we got more detailed. But starting here was important to build a one-company view of the Zipcar experience.

Then every year we would create a roadmap using the eco-system visual. Each year we would start with certain themes to focus on. Inside of each theme was the customer experience to be improved or heightened and why, the development, investment, and initiatives. This also included the financial impact and cost to the operation.

We used this singular format consistently every quarter and prior to planning to align and focus and make the work real and tangible.

3: BUILD A CUSTOMER LISTENING PATH.

Seek Input and Customer Understanding, Aligned to the Customer Journey.

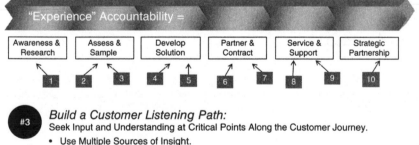

Build a Customer Listening Path:
Seek Input and Understanding at Critical Points Along the Customer Journey.
- Use Multiple Sources of Insight.
- Tell the Story of Customers' Lives.
- Unite Decision-Making and Focus.

Competency 3 unites your organization to build a one-company listening system that is constantly refreshed to tell the story of your customers' experience, guided by the customer journey framework. Feedback volunteered from customers as they interact with you, survey and social feedback, ethnography, and other sources of gathered input are assembled into one complete picture, presenting customer perception and value, stage by stage. This alignment of multiple sources of feedback focuses and galvanizes the organization to focus on key areas of improvement connected to customer growth, driving greater results and greater understanding of this work.

The role of the CCO is to engage leaders and the organization to want to be a part of one-company storytelling to unite decision-making and drive cross-company focus and action. That's why I call this competency as building a customer *'listening path*.

With this book, you'll be able to evaluate your current listening system to determine how to evolve to the comprehensive customer listening path of competency two. This will enable you to utilize multiple sources of information to move your company past survey-score addiction, to customer experience storytelling - prompting caring about customers' lives, and improvements that earn the right to growth.

 **Aggregating Insights To Interest Even the CFO**

Graham Atkinson
Chief Marketing and Customer Experience Officer
Walgreens

Graham Atkinson, is Chief Marketing and Customer Experience Officer at Walgreens, the largest drug-retailing chain in the United States, with responsibility for the full customer experience/relationship, including loyalty.

What I first encountered at Walgreens was that the stores were receiving a simplistic survey report with results by store. Often it gave them results from only 20 to 30 customers with only the survey score numeric. There was very little if any commentary behind the score. They might receive a few ad hoc comments. As you could guess, from these results, store managers could easily explain or rationalize bad results away.

Then, in our leadership meetings, we had a monthly report-out from sales and marketing. In this meeting there were just two lines of information reported on that applied to customers: the exit store survey results and the competitive results. One meeting's discussion on these results elicited an almost cathartic conversation, which opened the door to change.

We didn't really understand what this customer number meant or the impact. One of the first things we did to put meat on the bones of this information was to understand what we had in terms of tools and processes and start to build out a robust listening system with understanding and meaning behind the data we were gathering.

Within my first six months, we rebuilt our approach to give each store higher response rates with more credible feedback that was harder to refute, we built a program to identify how each store was performing to encourage a friendly horse-race among stores, and we did the heavy lifting for store managers to identify a few key things per store to focus on.

Over time, we created a central repository of multiple categories of listening feedback and turned it into a consistent scorecard on business performance. We also looked at behavioral loyalty so we could connect to improvements that would drive a return on investment. With analytics we were able to show how behaviors changed over time and how we needed to achieve different results to achieve customer-buying patterns that drive growth. Importantly, this was not just a rudimentary part of our leadership meetings—but presented as important as the report-out of financial results.

4: PROACTIVE EXPERIENCE RELIABILITY & INNOVATION.

Know Before Customers Tell You, Where Experiences Are Unreliable.
Deliver Consistent and Desired Experiences.

"Experience" Accountability =

1 2 3 4 5 6 7 8 9 10

Proactive Experience Reliability & Innovation:
Build the ability to predict performance, rebuild and innovate at key touchpoints.
Make customer experience development as important as product development.

Competency 4 builds out your "Revenue Erosion Early-Warning Process." We need leaders to care about operational performance in processes that impact priority moments in your customers' journey with you. These are the intersection points that impact customer decisions to stay, leave, buy more, and recommend you to others.

This is where you build your discipline to know *before customers tell you* if your operation is reliable or unreliable in experience delivery in the moments that matter most. The role of the CCO is to drive executive appetite for wanting to know about these interruptions in customers' lives, simplifying how they are delivered, and facilitating a one-company response to these key operational performance areas. It is to facilitate the competency of building a deliberate process for customer experience improvement that rivals the clarity and processes that most companies have for product development.

With this book, you will be able to evaluate how proactive your efforts are today in uniting leadership focus to identify and provide resources to improve priority customer experiences. You will receive information so that you can engage leaders in working with the silos to pull out the few critical metrics they should care about with as much rigor as they care about achieving sales goals. And you will gain a perspective from CCOs on how they built a path for embedding the competency of focus, capacity creation, and reward for one-company experience improvement.

Real Time Performance Visibility to Improve Customer Experience

Lambert Walsh
Vice President & General Manager, Global Services, Adobe

Lambert Walsh is Vice President and General Manager at Adobe, where he leads Adobe's efforts to retain and grow long-term relationships with customers and partners across all segments and lines of business. He has led customer success at Adobe since 2007.

At Adobe, we now have performance indicators that leaders across Adobe are accountable to, that build a connection between core system performance and delivering exceptional customer experiences with our services. Typical Software as a Service (SaaS) operational metrics around availability and uptime remain important, but they are internal metrics about how we are doing. Additional quality of service indicators will measure how we are performing in relation to what customers need in real time. For example, we may see that a system is up and running but a subset of customers may be experiencing disruption in performance, impeding tasks they want to perform. When we look at only the traditional system performance we risk getting a false positive of our performance and the customers' experience. With additional measures that reflect exactly what customers are seeing we can make adjustments in real time to ensure that we deliver the best experience possible.

5: LEADERSHIP, ACCOUNTABILITY & CULTURE

*Leadership Behaviors Required for Embedding the Five Competencies.
Enabling Employees to Deliver Value.*

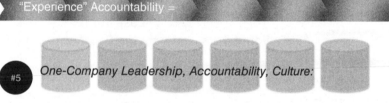

"Experience" Accountability =

#5   *One-Company Leadership, Accountability, Culture:*

Decisions and Operational Actions That Steer the Company Toward Customer-Driven Growth. United Leadership Behavior to Connect the Silos and Enable People to Act.

This is your "prove it to me" competency. For this work to be transformative and stick, it must be more than a customer manifesto. Commitment to customer-driven growth is proven with actions and choices. To emulate culture, people need examples. They need proof.

Culture must be proven with decisions and operational actions that are deliberate in steering how a company will and will not treat customers and employees. Competency five puts into practice united leadership behaviors to enable and earn sustainable customer asset growth. It focuses them on what *they will* and *will not* do to grow the business.

The role of the CCO is to work with the leadership team in building the consistent behaviors, decision-making, and company engagement that will prove to the organization that leaders are united in their commitment to earn the right to customer-driven growth.

You must move beyond the customer manifesto and translate the commitment to actions that people understand and can emulate. That's what competency five helps you to accomplish for your organization. In this book you will receive specific examples of a set of leadership actions that are foundational for the success of a customer experience transformation. And you will be provided with examples from chief customer officers on how they united their company's leadership in these critical actions. You will have the information to determine how to engage as a leadership team and where the critical roadblocks are that you must tackle.

Building Trust to Scale the Business

Tish Whitcraft
Chief Customer Officer
OpenX

Tish Whitcraft is Chief Customer Officer at OpenX, responsible for the partner experience and all revenue growth and retention. OpenX is a global leader in web and mobile advertising technology that optimizes the economic potential of digital media companies through advertising technology.

In a lot of organizations we put too many rules, policies, and frameworks in place, thinking that these will make a scalable experience. But a scalable experience occurs when we begin giving people the ability to make the right decisions. At OpenX, for example, we learned that we had to give account managers permission to make decisions to grow and scale the business.

One of the things we did was to simply begin having regular weekly meetings with account managers to enforce and go through specific customer issues they were having. We'd have them recommend what they thought should be done—and then give them the authority to just do it. Simple, right? But somewhere along the way someone didn't give them permission to make decisions. So they thought that was a rule they had to follow. And they stopped taking action and started asking first. And that got in the way of solving customer issues and creating value. It impeded growth and our ability to scale.

We also work deliberately to show customers that we have confidence in our own people and trust their decisions. We are always in meetings with customers—so we showcase their account manager as the one who owns the decisions on the account. If we make them get approval on everything—then the customer will see their account manager as a paper pusher they have to go around to get a decision.

The Five Competencies Build Your Customer-Driven Growth Engine

When these five competencies are embedded into the organization with committed leadership behavior, they are so clear that they become *the work* of the organization. There is no difference between the "customer" work and the "real" work. The five competencies connect to growth, and they shift attitudes to caring about and improving customer lives.

These five competencies unite the organization to identify and improve customer priorities with most impact. Today, surveys come out, and silos react to them. Research is done and they react. Products are developed with varying degrees of customer understanding. Everything is a distinct project without an overarching framework. Work streams begin without lines of sight to each other.

These competencies are designed with a clear connection to one another so that over time you have a repeatable and deliberate customer-driven growth engine. And please keep this in mind: the goal is that you build this *over time*. The customer leadership executive's role is to engage the organization to phase the build-out so that it sticks.

Five Competencies = Engine for Growth

1   HONOR AND MANAGE CUSTOMERS AS ASSETS
Know the Growth or Loss of Customers and Care About the 'WHY?'

2   ALIGN AROUND EXPERIENCE
Give Leaders a Framework for Guiding the Work of the Organization.
Unite Accountability as Customers Experience You. Not Down Your Silos.

3   BUILD A CUSTOMER LISTENING PATH
Seek Input and Customer Understanding, Aligned to the Customer Journey.

4   PROACTIVE EXPERIENCE RELIABILITY & INNOVATION
Know Before Customers Tell You, Where Experiences Are Unreliable.
Deliver Consistent and Desired Experiences.

5   LEADERSHIP, ACCOUNTABILITY & CULTURE
Leadership Behaviors Required for Embedding the Five Competencies.
Enabling Employees to Deliver Value.

Over time, one of this engine's most potent impacts is in prioritizing investments for customer-driven growth by shifting the annual planning process. Instead of starting with the silos, leaders start with the customers' lives, identify priorities, and then determine collectively the investments to improve them to earn the right to growth. Without alignment among your executive team to regularly review the customer journey that this engine affords, investments are not fully optimized. Tactical actions are budgeted and implemented by silo, but complete customer experiences that drive growth are not improved. Rinse and repeat.

State of the Customer Report

Claire Burns
Chief Customer Officer
MetLife

Claire Burns is Chief Customer Officer at MetLife. She drives the customer-centricity strategy and actions to build customer empathy and improve the experience of purchasing, maintaining, and enhancing customer coverage with MetLife. MetLife, Inc., is a global provider of insurance, annuities, and employee benefit programs.

As we go into our planning cycle we prepare the organization with a "State of the Customer" report. In this report we walk through what has improved and the lingering issues.

- We identify highlights and priorities by customer journeys specific to regions or countries.
- In the report we synthesize the customer experience for the past year, gathering insight from multiple sources: trended complaints, inbound feedback from the web and call centers, social media feedback, operational performance, and survey results.
- We identify "the top five-problems" list to be tackled by market area and the biggest success achieved in the current year.
- We also identify the two to three company-wide priorities we need to tackle.

Finally we provide a decision guideline—of what to do and what not to do to customers across the journey as they plan their actions.

If you're in the fray of silo-based reactivity to customer issues, these five competencies will help to emancipate you from those fire drills. For the CCO currently in the role, they will help you accelerate this work with clarity and leadership alignment. And for leadership teams, boards and newly appointed customer leadership executives, these five competencies will help you to begin the role and the work effectively, cutting years off your learning curve.

No matter which path you are on now, these five competencies will clarify and accelerate your work and elevate it to connect to business growth. The engine built from these five competencies gives you an organized and phased approach for investing in and building reliable experiences around the products and services you build. Within each of these five competencies are operational mechanics and cultural actions required to drive the transformation of doing this work for the right reasons, and with the impact of "earning the right" to customer growth.

The Five Competencies Connect to Tell the Story of Your Customers' Lives

These five competencies connect to tell the story of your customers' lives as they traverse your business. They begin with the outcome of the experience, which is how the customer asset grew or diminished (Competency 1). They organize listening, feedback, and organizational and experience reliability by stage of the experience, uniting actions to imagine and improve complete customer experiences, rather than independently driven silo-based actions (Competency 2 and 3). And they remove what I consider the Achilles' heel of customer experience, the lack of regular accountability for experience and inconsistent leadership behaviors and actions (Competencies 4 and 5).

As you build out these five competencies, your role as the customer leadership executive is to connect them to be the storyteller. Tell stories that move customers off spreadsheets, engage people personally in customers' lives, and compel prioritized and focused action. Tell the story of how your customer experience impacted customers' lives and business growth. In chapter two, you'll find more detail on how the five competencies connect in storytelling to reveal emerging opportunities for customer experience improvement and innovation.

You Can Stage the Competencies to Meet Your Timing and Priorities

There is a term that I am sure you have heard. It is connected to a major reason for customer experience transformation failure. And that is 'boiling the ocean' by taking on too much too fast, with multiple parts of the organization translating and taking action independently. My suggestion is to learn and understand the five competencies. But then stair-step actions for embedding the five competencies. Don't "boil the ocean" with an overwhelming implementation plan.

Here are the three methods we find to be most successful.

1. **Break the five competencies down into crawl-walk-run action steps.** For example, in Competency 1, Honoring and Managing Customers as Assets, don't wait until you have all the data perfectly aligned and automated until you roll this out. Start with the data you have now, even if it means manually building spreadsheets.

2. **Improve priority experiences while developing the five competencies.** Unite leaders on the identification of the priority customer experience touchpoints. Learn how to work as one-company to solve and improve them.

3. **Prove out the process before expanding.** I had a client who wanted to embed the five competencies in three countries simultaneously. My recommendation was to rollout version 1 of the five competencies in one country first, working out the kinks and gaining experience and relevant examples. Instead, there was pressure to go broad and go fast. You can predict how that ended.

The Five Competencies Answer the Question "What Do You Do?"

When I worked in the role of CCO, it drove me crazy to receive the question, *"What* do you do?" Now, my clients receive it. These five competencies will answer that question and define the CCO role. Each of the five competencies, with their explicit outcomes, clarify what the CCO function does and what it enables the leaders and organization to do.

By engaging the organization in building the repeatable cycle of the five customer leadership competencies, the organization can unite, understand and care about customers' lives, and pool resources to focus on what is most important. This repeatable cycle will drive growth. The chief customer officer, in short, is the architect of this customer-driven growth.

Throughout the course of this book, you will receive information, tools, sustenance and support to enable you and your leadership team to customize and build your version of a customer-driven growth engine.

How We've Elevated My Role and This Work

Pete Winemiller
Senior Vice President of Guest Relations
NBA's Oklahoma City Thunder

Pete Winemiller is Senior Vice President of Guest Relations for the NBA's Oklahoma City Thunder. He is charged with creating repeat customers in a business environment where you cannot control the level of success on the basketball court, but you can control what happens in the stands.

For the Thunder organization, the guest experience is a pillar of our business on equal footing with other departments, such as sales and marketing. And here's why: The nature of our business is that we can't control the level of success on the basketball court (the purchased product), but we can control what happens in the stands (the customer experience).

Even if the game outcome is not what we hope, the goal is that the overall guest experience will keep our fans coming back. That means our work is yoked to the other departments in driving the economics of our business.

We are fortunate to have a leadership group that values the guest experience in equal weight to the other economic drivers of our business. In other businesses, the customer-experience role does not always have a seat at the same leadership table as marketing or finance. In our organization, we all are committed to the idea that the guest experience is essential to meet our overall business goals.

Summary

The power of these five competencies is how they connect to drive clarity for customer experience transformation and the role of the CCO:

1. The five competencies establish an engine for driving customer growth.
2. The CCO facilitates the construct of the engine, engaging leaders and employees throughout the company.
3. The engine enables one-company customer growth behavior and actions.
4. Without this united engine, activities go back to being ruled by squeaky wheel issues, executive-driven one-off action items, and silo-by-silo priorities.

ACTION LAB   **CURRENT STATE: FIVE COMPETENCIES**

Below please find an audit I conduct with my clients at the beginning of each coaching engagement to determine how much work has been completed in each of the five competencies. I encourage you to use this audit as a tool to clarify the CCO role as guiding

(continued)

(*continued*)

the company to build out these competencies, and to clarify what you can achieve by embedding the five competencies into how you operate your business.

If your results suggest that you are "early" in some activities within the competencies, you are in good company. The early stage is in many cases the outcome of silos working hard (even after many years of survey work or focus)—but working hard *separately*. That is why the five competencies are powerful ... because they create an engine to unite leaders and your organization.

Competency 1: Honor and Manage Customers as Assets *Current State Assessment*	
Description	**Where Are We Now?**
Culture Do we stress and actively pursue how we are managing the asset of the Customer growth or loss? Do we highlight where we are in losing or gaining Customers as key talking points in meetings within the organization?	EARLY ADVANCED MATURE
Data Enabling Have we identified all the data sources that need to connect to consistently and confidently measure and manage the growth or loss of the Customer asset across the organization?	EARLY ADVANCED MATURE
Wanting to know WHY? Are we actively anxious and passionate about why Customers are leaving—do we want to know what operationally we did to drive departure? Do we personally talk to Customers who have left—not as a research exercise but to know them, and as an operational call to action?	EARLY ADVANCED MATURE

Competency 2: Align Around Experience *Current State Assessment*	
Description	**Where Are We?**
<u>Alignment Around Experience</u> Do we have consensus on how to define the experience we deliver to our Customers—holistically as they would describe it? Have we agreed on the number of journeys? Do we have consensus on the stages of the experience?	EARLY ADVANCED MATURE
<u>Move from Silo-based Actions to Customer Priorities</u> Have we mapped the touchpoints to know which are most critical to a) driving revenue, b) forming a relationship/bond, c) rescuing Customers at risk, and d) retaining and growing share of wallet?	EARLY ADVANCED MATURE
Have we done the research and work to know what Customers value most, emotionally what drives them so that we can build differentiated actions? Are we focusing on the right things?	EARLY ADVANCED MATURE

Competency 3: Build a Customer Listening Path *Current State Assessment*	
Description	**Where Are We?**
<u>Aided Listening</u> *(we initiate request for feedback)* Is the survey score the big focus? Do we put the right emphasis on understanding what is causing experience issues, or are we focused on the score? Do we bring in other insights to inform and drive action, or do we tend to react to survey scores in isolation?	EARLY ADVANCED MATURE
<u>Real-time Unaided Listening</u> *(customers volunteer feedback)* Have we identified high volume 'listening pipes' (complaints, social, etc.) to know real-time issues/opportunities? Are they organized into consistent categories so they roll up to a trend? Do we watch customer behaviors and use that information as a source of real-time information on customer experiences?	EARLY ADVANCED MATURE
<u>Telling the Story of Customers' Lives</u> Are we aggregating multiple sources of insights to tell a balanced story of customer experience issues and innovative opportunities? Do we align customer insights to the stages of the customer journey? Do we practice 'experiential' listening, where people take actions we require customers to do, to understand customers' lives?	EARLY ADVANCED MATURE

Competency 4: Proactive Experience Reliability and Innovation *Current State Assessment*	
Description	**Where Are We?**
<u>Rescuing High-Value Customers at Risk</u> Are we deliberate about knowing which Customers need follow-through and when? Do we have a system to do this follow-through? Do we have skilled people? Are we reaching out to Customers, not just from call centers, but from throughout the organization?	EARLY ADVANCED MATURE
<u>One-Company Experience Improvement</u> Do we do a lot of "one offs" fixing issues one Customer at a time…or do we also fix the company? Do we focus on the key priorities or does every silo pick their own? Do we have an accountability process around the identification, cross-functional teaming, and metrics for solving this issues? Have we embedded a competency for customer experience improvement throughout the company?	EARLY ADVANCED MATURE
<u>Experience Innovation</u> Beyond resolving reliability issues, are we actively understanding evolving customer needs and values to inspire innovation? Have we built a customer experience development process and competency that rivals in its importance, the new product development process?	EARLY ADVANCED MATURE

Competency 5: One-Company Leadership, Accountability, Culture *Current State Assessment*	
Description	**Where Are We?**
<u>Leadership Communication, Action, Beliefs</u> Are leader united in how they communicate about improving customers' lives? Do they drive cross-company collaboration, accountability, and metrics, to enable reliable customer experiences? Do they make decisions that honor customers as assets?	EARLY ADVANCED MATURE
Do leaders actively engage across the organization to listen and understand what is going on with Customers and employees charged with delivering an experience to them? Do they kill "stupid rules" getting in the way of honoring employees & customers?	EARLY ADVANCED MATURE
<u>Enabling Employees to Deliver Value.</u> Is clarity of purpose for serving Customers' lives understood and translated to everyone's work? Does that clarity guide hiring decisions? Does it guide investment in skills and competency development to enable our people to deliver value to customers?	EARLY ADVANCED MATURE

Unite Leadership to Achieve Customer-Driven Growth

The five competencies will establish clarity and value for the role of the chief customer officer (CCO). However, it is attitudinal shifts in leadership thinking and behavior that will determine how well they can be embedded to successfully transform your business. Many factors related to leadership and culture will impact your ability to achieve role clarity, unite leaders, and make the five competencies stick.

The CCO needs to be a sleuth, uncovering and navigating agendas and factors that slow down and can threaten the work, especially if some leaders question its connection to business growth (when we really feel like we're pushing that rock up the hill).

My goal here is to help you build or rebuild traction as quickly and effectively as possible. The difference between thriving and flaming out as a CCO comes down to moving this work quickly from chasing survey scores to driving growth, leadership team clarity for your role and their required involvement, and knowing what kind of corporate sandbox you're involved in transforming.

Supporting Your CEO's Legacy

With increasing frequency executives want this work to be their legacy. They want to leave an indelible mark on the organization that while it was in his or her care, they championed and enabled customer-driven growth.

In your role as customer leadership executive, embedding the five customer leadership competencies will create clarity for building that legacy. When these become part of how the company conducts itself, leadership attitudes for the work will shift. It won't feel "layered on." Annual planning will begin with reviewing customers' lives. Leaders will change their goals from "getting loyalty or a survey score" to earning the right to customer-driven growth.

CCOs reach out to me as they are beginning in their roles, but also after they have been doing the work for a while, because the work has stalled. Often those who are stopped in their tracks or who have made incrementally smaller steps (staying in the role of fix-it person, for example) are those who did not have a chance to work through and embed the elements outlined in this chapter which are necessary for role adoption and success.

In this chapter, as in the rest that follow, you'll benefit from years of experience in pushing the customer rock up the hill from my CCO clients in addition to other customer leadership executives doing this work globally. These benefits come in the form of lessons learned, shared openly in their own words, in the "My Rock, My Story" vignettes peppered throughout this book. You'll recognize your own life and work in these stories.

Here are the cornerstones of a successful transformation:

- **Focus on Growth and Customers as Assets**. *Remove Survey Score Addiction.*
- **Identify Your Power Core**. *Know What Helps or Hinders the Work.*
- **Unite Leadership and Connect Talk to Action**. *Eliminate the "Baloney" Factor.*
- **Tell the Story of Customers' Lives**. *Care Why Customers Stay or Go.*
- **Improve the Business Engine**. *Earn the Right to Do This Work.*

This chapter will cover each of these key elements in detail, to prepare you for success in this role, and give you the foundation for successfully embedding the five competencies.

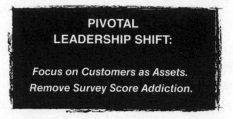

Uniting the leadership team in the purpose of delivering one-company experiences and connecting them to business growth is the goal of the Chief Customer Officer. This pivotal shift will occur when you can establish the growth or loss of the customer asset as a critical report card on the experience delivered, and compel leaders to care why your customers stay or go.

Pivotal Leadership Shift: Elevate Customers as Assets

Customers as assets measure the impact of the end-to-end experiences of your business. It measures what customers actually *did* (via their behaviors) versus what they *say* they are going to do (via surveys). Measuring customers as assets illuminates how customers voted with their feet to (a) stay or go, (b) get more or less from you, or (c) bring others to you. Most important, it shifts conversations about this work from the internally driven attention to achievement of sales or survey scores, to caring about customers' lives. To caring about why customer behavior changed as a result of their journey with you.

Engaging the Board to Care About the "Why?"

Hilary Noon
Vice President, Marketplace Insight and Experience
The American Cancer Society

Hilary Noon is Vice President of Marketplace Insight and Experience at the American Cancer Society. In her role she is the thought leader responsible for driving customer-focused strategy at the C-Suite and Business Unit owner levels of the organization.

We just proposed a new success metric to our board to give them an indication of the health of our donor portfolio. While we are still working through the particulars, the goal is to show in very simple terms the net effect of donor acquisition, retention, and attrition behaviors for a reporting period. We will examine how many donors we lost compared with how many new donors we brought in, viewed against our existing base of donors. This will give us a net donor growth or decline metric. We will also show any shifting behavior within our donors such as movement to different donor levels, or lapses in donating. We are starting to get very high interest in this. As expected, we are having a lot of healthy debate about what we are going to show and how.

As we do this, we've also found that it is important to pay attention to the "why" behind the numbers. When a dashboard is first presented to a board or other leadership group, the tendency is to focus on the numbers and graphs independently of one another. Few people strive to have a discussion about how the information works together to tell the story of the "why" behind something like donor growth or loss. To help stimulate this kind of discussion, we are planning to show the highest level metric to the board, which includes the outcome information. We will give another level of detail to our committees and staff leadership, which will include the drivers of donor growth. They can use that information to focus on understanding the "why" and determine how best to act on it.

Your opportunity is to gain leadership attention to this simple definition of success. To create desire for knowing and managing customer asset performance with the same rigor applied to sales, revenue, and IBITA performance. Honoring and managing the customer asset leads directly to results leaders care about.

Customers as Assets Is an Attitude Shift, Not a Dashboard

Chapter three will provide you with a toolkit to start to build your customized version of customer asset metrics. But I can't emphasize enough its importance as an attitudinal shift you must achieve with company's leaders before you start doing the math to build this metric. Besides uniting leaders to build common definitions and data to establish a one-company articulation of the growth and loss of the customer asset, to be successful as a transformative action this must be accompanied by a shift in how leaders communicate the success of the business. They must become fearless enough to start meetings connecting the efforts of the entire organization to the growth or loss of this asset. Did we, all together, earn the right to growth?

Customer asset metrics when embraced and communicated consistently across leadership shed a new light on why you are in business. In their simplicity, they drive action. You either keep (or lose or grow) customers or you don't. Caring about that will change your leaders' behaviors. It will help you transform your business.

Remove Survey Score Addiction by Adding Customer Asset Metrics

So often when executives talk about commitment to customer experience, they connect it primarily to survey score results. That is because, in the absence of other simple ways to measure progress, such as a united one-company tracking of customer growth or loss, that score is the one quantifiable measure of success. Getting good scores leads conversations rather than discussion of customers' lives.

There is a disquieting conflict between the focus on customers' lives that surveys are intended to improve and the organizational behaviors that ensue from trying to get "good" survey results. I've seen too many conversations about results devoid of conversations about actual customers.

The end game becomes the score. Spreadsheets mire leaders down in calculations driven by survey results and keep them focused on earning higher scores. So embedded is this addiction to survey results that many clients tell me that sending out the survey, waiting for results, and trying to get "lift" on the score is the their complete customer strategy.

As detailed in the upcoming chapters on the five competencies, surveys have an important place in this work as part of the information provided in the five-competency framework to give a balanced story of customers' lives. This balance enables leaders and the organization to step through the customer journey regularly—not only numerically but also experientially. It involves the company in understanding how what the company did or did not do impacted customer experiences and future behaviors, which grow or impede customer growth. Chapter five, "Building a Customer Listening Path," covers surveys and their function in this work in complete detail.

Elevating Customers as Assets Diminishes "Leap of Faith" for this Work

Let me ask you a question: Is your job focused on getting items fixed that emerge out of survey results? Are you seen as the fix-it person? If you are, then this work is still not thought of as a growth strategy. It's thought of as a cost to the business. It's seen as new work layered on top of the "real" work (we love that, don't we?). Which may be why your place on the CEO's meeting agenda moves down and down the page until sometimes it slips right off.

This lack of understanding of how to quantify success for customer-centric work drives survey score addiction. As a result the score becomes the standard bearer of success. And every silo is motivated to go to the dashboard to figure out what they can do to create "lift" on the part of the score that their operation impacts.

It is why your job may be ruled by it right now. The primary metrics used to indicate how well customers and partners are being treated are survey scores ... questions we asked customers after the fact about how we did. And how those scores stack up to competitors.

Using survey scores alone to quantify and drive action puts this work (and your role) in the "leap of faith" category. The connection between improved scores and improved growth is not always clear. That means "customer focus" may be a top agenda item of the organization, but it's not easily quantified. So leaders take a leap of faith to do the work because it's the right thing to do.

You can end this cycle by engaging leaders to elevate customers as the asset of your business. And by creating clarity that your role is to work with them to unite the organization in growing this asset.

Fatigued by Survey Score Chasing

Taylor Rhodes
*President & CEO. Previously Chief Customer Officer
Rackspace*

Taylor Rhodes is President and CEO of Rackspace. He was previously Senior Vice President and Chief Customer Officer. Rackspace is a leader in managed cloud, delivering open technologies and powering hundreds of thousands of customers worldwide.

What I am finding is that in our maturity of using surveys for many years, score chasing can drive fatigue in improvement efforts. When our survey was new and fresh, understanding the score worked to galvanize people and give a target. But now that we are mature in our process, it is fatiguing.

The emphasis should be on understanding customers and taking action rather than being motivated by increasing the score. Rather than focusing on the score as the thing to watch and see value in, we want people to learn and be invigorated by using the verbatim comments to understand, at a more human customer level, what are the issues.

For example, we use these with product managers to show what is trending. At this point, we focus more on challenging "Rackers" to identify the things our customers are talking about and if they love or hate them. We still recognize greatness, but we recognize different things—the behaviors. Did someone listen to their customer and solve the problem? Getting good at using this verbatim feedback from surveys, from regular interactions, from within our product usage and on social media is where we need to improve.

At the end of the day, our highest reward from customers is did they stay with us and continue to realize value, and did they buy more and tell others? To that end, we are tying growth of our install base, the customer asset to people's bonus and career path as our ultimate goal. This moves the score as one indicator of how we are performing, but not the ultimate motivating factor for our work.

Just today I was in a meeting with the leadership team of a manufacturing company client. This quote came from our discussion of managing customers as assets as a shared responsibility of the leadership team: "We are so product oriented, we think of the product as the asset of our business. This is a critical shift because it causes us to think about the customer, the life of the person buying the product. This totally changes what we think of as success."

That was a great moment. Of course there is much work ahead of that team now to quantify how to track and agree on the growth and loss of the customer asset. But the idea is now there and the transformation begins.

Before we leave this conversation, ponder this:

- What would change in your company if every executive meeting started with "Did we earn the right to customer growth?"
- Then move to specifics. In each segment of your customer base, how many new customers were acquired, in whole numbers—in volume and value?
- Next, by segment of your customer base, how many customers did we lose, in whole numbers—in volume and value?
- And, most important, WHY? What did we do to grow or shrink this asset? Across the entire operation, not just in sales or service, but as a result of the overall experience delivered?

This is a lot different from looking at survey scores and discussing getting "lift" on a number without discussing your customers' lives, isn't it? And that's the power of elevating and honoring customers as assets. It lays the groundwork to enable the work because it connects it to ROI and growth. It unites leaders.

Embracing customers as assets shifts the attitude of leaders and ultimately the organization, because the purpose is to earn the right to growth by improving the lives of customers. When you improve their lives, the high scores will follow. They will. But the shift is to start the work with the customer's life, not the score. And that is no small shift.

Chapter three is fully dedicated to the competency of customers as assets. In this chapter there are more specifics about how to go about this transformation with your organization and leadership team. You will find the following sections in all the chapters on the five competencies:

- **Action Lab:** Tools to put immediately into use
- **My Rock, My Story:** True life stories from fellow CCOs

ACTION LAB   VISUAL CUSTOMER ASSET STORY

We have found that sometimes the first way to get traction is to get acknowledgment that there is work to be done. As you may experience, retention rates or survey scores may not be telling the story of growth or loss of the customer base.

With several clients, to get the point across to the C-Suite that customer growth was eroding, we wanted to demonstrate visually that they were losing more customers than they were gaining. So we came up with a pretty unique idea with marbles. We determined the mathematical equation for the number of customers a single marble would represent. Then we showed them two jars of marbles. One was filled with marbles that represented new customers, and another was filled to represent lost customers. The jar of "lost customers" had more marbles. We were also able to figure in customer "value" to visually give

(continued)

(*continued*)

an accurate depiction of the impact of having to refill the jar of marbles.

This got attention. We were able to prove that while we were hitting sales goals, we weren't growing. Incremental growth had to come from existing customers by delivering an experience they would want to have again and tell others about.

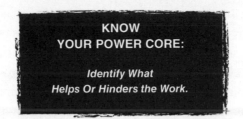

**KNOW
YOUR POWER CORE:**

*Identify What
Helps Or Hinders the Work.*

What's funny when you write a book like this is that you spend a lot of time alone (me in crummy pajamas my husband hates), trying to decode complex issues. That's how it was figuring out and writing about the power core. It was the hardest chapter in the first Chief Customer Officer book because I had to decode why we can hit a wall in this work. *Why could I make traction in some companies but not budge the work an inch in others?* The answer came in establishing that every company has a power core that helps or hinders the work.

Determining the company power core has helped every one of my clients advance the adoption of their role and aid in embedding the five competencies. It is their decoder for understanding the political barriers and enablers to their success. It's one of the "aha" moments I hear from people who read and use that book as a tool. Understanding your company power core is going to tell you a lot about how to move forward.

When I work with companies now, we always determine the company power core and measure its impact in driving the corporate agenda. This yields an immediate understanding of the complexity and scale of the job required to integrate customer experience and customer profitability into the business model. Here's the information to diagnose your power core.

Knowing the Power Core = Knowing How to Get Traction

The complexity and scale of work required to build your customer-driven growth engine will be affected by the strength of the power core and how it drives priorities. Most companies have a predominant power core. Frequently it is the strongest skill set in the company or the most comfortable to senior executives. Because executives know the power core best, people gravitate to perform in that area where they know they are most assuredly met with acknowledgment and reward. The power core can be the most influential in directing the silos and is one of the biggest determinants of how success, metrics, recognition, and company growth are defined.

The idea of the power core was born from the varying experiences I had in achieving results and engaging across the silos as I traversed from Lands' End to Mazda, then Coldwell Banker, Allstate, and Microsoft in my roles as CCO. I was hitting different roadblocks but for different reasons at each organization.

I was spoiled from my first years in this work at Lands' End, reporting to founder Gary Comer, because nearly everything we built was created from the customer perspective out. In that period we grew from $100,000 in sales to over $1 billion. Performance metrics and recognition were grounded in how we delivered on the promises and guarantees made to customers. When we went public, a major part of our messaging (delivered by yours truly at the age of 26) to the financial analysts assessing our business was establishing the link between how we treated customers and our business growth.

This was not the case when I moved to the automotive industry and observed that the power core was not the customer but product and sales. During my time in that industry, the economy was shrinking, and the automotive product market was shifting and on the cusp of understanding customer value and retention. If I wanted to talk about customer loyalty, it needed to be about a certain vehicle, not overall brand loyalty. To get attention, it was best to first provide sales numbers, followed by the customer retention and repurchase information.

The lessons from my experiences and those of my clients continue to ring true: know the source, methods of operating, and priorities of those with their fingers on the power button. Below is an example of how this was done at Audi, to gain a commitment to invest in culture activities.

Proving a Return-On-Investment on Culture Activities

Jeri Ward
Director of Customer Experience, Audi of America, LLC
Audi

Jeri Ward is Director of Customer Experience at Audi of America, LLC, where she holds the senior leadership position for customer experience strategy, insights, and transformation across the enterprise.

We knew we needed to create fans internally with our people and dealerships in order to create fans with customers. To achieve this, we planned a cultural engagement that swept across the United States in an eight-city, sixteen-show tour with live immersion events for Audi and dealership employees. The goal was to unite everyone in our mission.

This cultural engagement plan had to be signed-off by our colleagues in Germany. It was a challenge to sell the return on investment of a cultural engagement project because it was like nothing we had ever done before; it was one of the less familiar aspects in our plan, and one of the largest investments. However, we knew it was going to make a difference, so we had to figure out how to sell the Return on investment (ROI).

To sell the ROI we connected our company's strong pride in what we stand for with the fact that there was at the time a gap between our beliefs for our company and how customers perceived and trusted us in the marketplace. To tell this story, we peeled back customer data from both buyers and rejecters to understand why people were or were not turning to the Audi brand. Dealer treatment was one of the high drivers of rejection. Those behavioral or attitudinal issues showed up as lack of trust in sales, service, or financing staffers. One of our most galvanizing data points was the impression that people interacting with customers were considered "rude" when compared to a key competitor's. That got the attention of key management. There was agreement from all of us that this was not consistent with our brand values and it was alarming that this was a perception in the marketplace.

Having proven the need for this new work, we then identified that increasing loyalty and diminishing rejecters starts with changing the behaviors that were driving customers away. If we reduced rejecters to the brand, and retained more loyal owners, then there would be a positive return on investment in this work. We made our case. We received the go-ahead.

(continued)

(continued)

The result was a three-month tour through the United States with our president and our executive team, sharing our mission with over 10,000 members of our U.S. Audi family from our dealerships, Audi employees, and vendor partners. The reaction from our people, at all levels, has been very positive. And better yet, it's working. We see it and hear about it from our customers. And every key performance indicator is on the rise, from customer satisfaction to loyalty to sales. Now there is demand for a sequel!

Six Common Power Cores

There are six common power cores we've seen with clients around the world. You'll likely find one of them to be the dominant factor in decision-making and direction in your company. You may also see another in a supporting second place of strength.

When a transformation begins without understanding the impact of the power core's pull on the agenda, it will usually impact speed and results. Understanding the strength and pull of your power core will frame the scope of work required to influence change. It will provide clarity on the approach to creating partnerships with leaders and in motivating people to change.

For example, it can be challenging to embed customer-driven competencies inside technology and product-driven companies. The customer experience process work—improving broken operational issues, key performance indicators, and so forth—are where efforts typically can gain momentum and establish a track for success within many industries. But with product power core companies, the starting point for gaining traction has to be adjusted. In these organizations, we often gain the greatest momentum when we focus first on partnering with product development to add value to them, using customer feedback and insights to improve the product.

Trying to advance this work through task forces will also be challenging if they are not in alignment with the priorities of the power core. Teams of people are assembled to solve a problem and there is agreement to begin the work. But when the work requires changes in process, accountability, metrics, and a reporting schedule assigned to the task, the backlash begins: "We don't report to you." "There's no time for this." "This won't leave time to make sales." On and on it goes. This is because the power core hasn't been asked to the dance.

When Product Development or Product Engineering Is Your Power Core

The product *is* the company in the eyes of the marketplace. Product development groups get the most resources and the most play, and they have the most power. Just look at the organization chart. Metrics are about new products, sizes of products, getting products out, speed of product development, and competitive progress of products in relation to competitors.

When Sales Is Your Power Core

You are a growth-acquisition-driven company. The quest for the sale pulls the weight in the company. In these organizations, people are motivated to make the numbers. Performance is frequently measured in short-term sales goals and targets. Sales targets are the strongest and most tracked corporate metrics. "Speed" sales are rewarded, even if they don't necessarily result in long-term customer profitability. Frequently the organization hasn't worked together to ensure that the after-sale experience delivers on the promise of the sale.

When Engineering or Information Technology Is Your Power Core

The explosion of SaaS Companies and continued growth of IT-based businesses have made the priorities of these groups the power core of their business, driving agendas, priorities, and investments. In addition, because the bulk of spending related to IT projects far exceeds other financial requirements, IT has been given an inordinate amount of power in determining the priorities of the organization—and not just in technology resources. It also has a loud voice in representing, selecting, and enabling IT-dependent projects across the organization. Technology leads the corporate agenda.

Often these spending requests come through annual planning without a prioritization lens to determine which are critical for customer asset growth and customer experience improvement, as they come in silo-by-silo. This compromises what should be a strategic IT strategy into a cluster of silo-driven pieces that may not cumulatively have the most powerful impact or make the most efficient use of resources.

How We Engage Our Engineers

Jeb Dasteel
Senior Vice President and Chief Customer Officer
Oracle

Jeb Dasteel is Senior Vice President and Chief Customer Officer at Oracle, where he is responsible for development and implementation of Oracle's strategy for maximizing the value of customers as a core company asset. This includes driving organizational focus on the success of our customers and harnessing that success to drive incremental revenue for Oracle through customer feedback, analytics, care, response, communications, customer marketing, and advocacy programs.

There are two traits that come through in everything we do at Oracle. We are a very engineering-centric organization and we take all forms of competition very seriously.

To drive customer centricity, we embrace the core of our engineering orientation and fierce competitive spirit. It's all about presenting people with comparative data that's actionable. I mean actionable for the business, for a particular organization, for a team, and for the individual. We make sure the data is relatable so that everyone can tie customer input to what they do. And the data is always comparative so that we play into our competitive nature.

For the engineering teams in particular, we use product scorecards to show how every characteristic of a product impacts the broader customer experience. The scorecards are effective because they establish one common framework and language for assessing and reacting to customer sentiment. The exact same concept applies to how we measure and compare services, relationship management, ease of doing business, and other aspects of the customer experience.

We provide our engineers with both the qualitative customer feedback—anecdotes, complaints, praise—and the quantitative data combined. All of this together gives us a complete "voice of the customer" perspective. Having rich data is great, but having the narrative from customers describing the effect we have on their business puts the data into the right context so that they can fully comprehend what they are building and improve on what and how they deliver.

Our engineers are one of many audiences we are constantly delivering customer loyalty, product effectiveness, and other data to throughout the company. We go from the macro, with the Oracle board of directors and executive committee, to the micro, with engineering teams, sales, support, and even back-office functions. As we have seen with engineering, it is making the data relevant by audience that has the greatest impact.

When Vertical Business Operations, Such As Insurance, Are Your Power Core

This power core is based on a particular competency related to an industry or function. The term *vertical power core* is used because deliverables to customers are akin to a vertical line of business highly focused on one particular area. We've all experienced the strong vertical disposition of the medical industry: some physicians are evolving, but many still define work by procedure rather than customer name ("I've got an appendectomy at eight, then tonsils at three"). This aligns with medical practitioner training: livers, hearts, the circulatory system, and so on. Bedside Manner 101, while not a part of the curriculum or considered a core competency, is slowly starting to show up on medical school curriculums.

The insurance industry is yet another vertical power core business. Most insurance companies have classically run their businesses to be proficient in the disciplines of actuarial calculations, policy development, claims execution, and other traditional areas of the insurance business. However, shifting consumer needs and demands and game-changing actions that started with Progressive and the heralded practices of USAA have prompted that industry to shift. The race is on to wrap a customer experience around the delivery of that insurance policy.

When Marketing Is Your Power Core

Marketing defines the tenor and tone of the relationship with customers. Brand at the advertising and messaging level is emphasized, but the implications for how to tie that to the experience can fall short. The opportunity is aligning the brand experience promised with the delivery of customer and employee experiences.

Translating the "brand promise" into how the company will conduct itself with employees and customers to stay true to that promise and operational alignment to execute on delivering the promise across the silos are often the gaps in the marketing power core company. As the role of marketing is evolving, new skill sets for uniting the organization in understanding and translating the brand promise operationally are required.

When the Customer Is Your Power Core

Company decisions start with clearly understanding what will deliver value to customers in the short and long term. Leaders are united in efforts to deliver a reliable and differentiated customer experience to drive the greatest amount of profitable customers. While silos exist, they are united with clarity of purpose in improving customers' lives. Planning and decision-making teams assemble for experience creation and delivery, not just silo-based projects. Employees are enabled to deliver value to customers and are also honored as assets of the company.

These companies began with the customer at their core. In a company with a customer power core, customer needs drive the overall plan for what's developed and delivered. As you can see in the following illustration, the Columbus Metropolitan Library not only has the customer at the core of their business, they organize to ensure that the customer focus is at the center of all of their activities. CCO Alison Circle described this structure as the way they are able to align everyone's decision-making lens around supporting and helping children to begin their lives on the right path and become lifelong readers and learners.

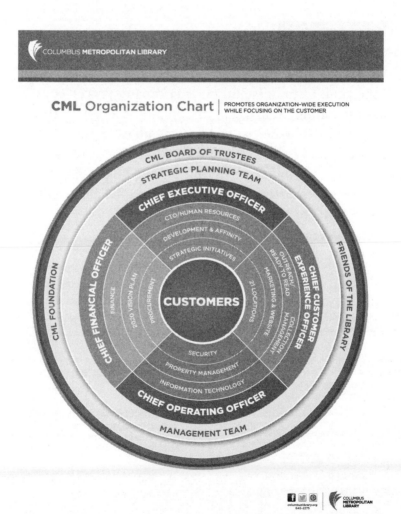

Customer Power Core: Columbus Metropolitan Library's Organization Chart

Other Emerging Power Cores

Other emerging power cores are finance, operations, and human resources. The point is to identify your company's power core and use that understanding to frame the scale of the work to integrate customer leadership and customer profitability management. The six that I identify in this section are simply the predominant ones. Regardless of what your power core is, it will have an impact on how you strategically address the work.

ACTION LAB　　WHAT IS YOUR POWER CORE?

Take the time to understand your company power core. If you are just beginning your work, understand the key partners who must see value in order to become steadfast partners with you. If you are leading the work and have hit some resistance, you may discover why by determining your company's power core. Identify your power core below to determine how and who to make sure you engage in this work.

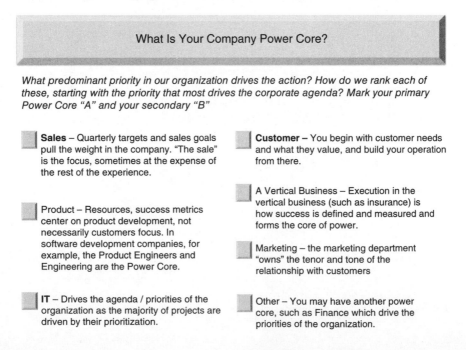

What Is Your Company Power Core?

What predominant priority in our organization drives the action? How do we rank each of these, starting with the priority that most drives the corporate agenda? Mark your primary Power Core "A" and your secondary "B"

Sales – Quarterly targets and sales goals pull the weight in the company. "The sale" is the focus, sometimes at the expense of the rest of the experience.

Product – Resources, success metrics center on product development, not necessarily customers focus. In software development companies, for example, the Product Engineers and Engineering are the Power Core.

IT – Drives the agenda / priorities of the organization as the majority of projects are driven by their prioritization.

Customer – You begin with customer needs and what they value, and build your operation from there.

A Vertical Business – Execution in the vertical business (such as insurance) is how success is defined and measured and forms the core of power.

Marketing – the marketing department "owns" the tenor and tone of the relationship with customers

Other – You may have another power core, such as Finance which drive the priorities of the organization.

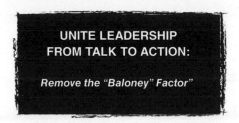

UNITE LEADERSHIP
FROM TALK TO ACTION:

Remove the "Baloney" Factor"

Culture is the action, not the words. It is consistent behaviors that give people direction on what to "model." It's decisions made and actions taken that prove that the customer commitment is real and not lip service. That it's not baloney.

How many years have you been doing this work? When did you begin to make progress? Your answer is probably directly connected to how engaged your leadership team is with you, when you engaged them, and how much they take personal ownership of this work with you.

A United Leadership Team Is Necessary to Move from Talk to Action

This transformation will only occur with consistent and united behaviors, communications, and actions practiced by leaders. Over the course of my career in this field since 1983, leaders have often asked me this question: *"Tell me what you need me to do to support your work."* This question is always intended to help, and it gets to the root of why this work often stalls out. The answer is:

- This must also be *your* work and the work of a united leadership team.
- The leadership team must model new behaviors in how they lead.
- Repeated and consistent messaging and actions must exist among leaders.
- Actions must be congruent with our stated commitment to customer-driven growth.

Uniting Leaders From Talk to Action

Kevin Thompson
Vice President Customer Experience and Development
Barney's New York

Kevin Thompson is Vice President of Customer Experience and Development at the luxury retailer Barneys New York. Kevin is responsible for managing the highest service standards across all company touch points, including stores, restaurants, e-commerce, and credit services, to create a seamless Omni-channel brand experience.

Our biggest challenge was in helping our stores and our people deliver a customer-centric experience. We have to make the experience go beyond buying an expensive handbag, to delivering moments where customers feel good about being in our stores and working with our people. Luxury retail has had to evolve along with the way that people want to shop and be treated while they are shopping. Our clients are always looking for the best product, but they are also looking for a shopping experience that adds value to that product once purchased. It is the memory of that experience that adds value.

In order for us to change the customer culture at Barneys New York, we have broken our work into five key "working" areas being developed as complete bodies of work, uniting multiple areas of our company within each. Teams are building-out experiences for the East and West Coast customer experiences, Omni-channel experience, customer segmentation, and end-to-end journeys, and overall customer experience strategy.

Each of the five working groups has a senior leader chairing with each team comprised of people from across all divisions with different points of view, to include all the dimensions of our business. The working groups are comprised of store managers, salespeople, and members of the merchant teams, marketing, e-commerce, and other operating areas. Each team is working on building-out the plans and actions recommended via a multiyear customer experience study and are presenting them to our CEO. Building these teams is changing our culture while also giving ownership and embedding the importance of cross-silo collaboration.

"Customer Culture" is talked about by many leaders but misunderstood by most organizations. That is because it is spoken of as a concept, rather than attached to deliberate behavior and consideration of customers' and employees' lives. Deliberate behaviors such as, "We will go to market only after these ten customer requirements are met." Or, "Every launch must meet these five conditions the field requires for success. We won't launch without them, no exceptions."

The role of the chief customer officer is to work with leaders to unite behavior. It is to unite actions to provide proof to the organization that this leadership team is committed to driving growth by improving customers' lives. Moving well past words, a deliberate and united set of actions and behaviors practiced in unison is required.

Three common categories of behavior are necessary as the leadership team works together to build out the five competencies. When these show up consistently they prove that a commitment to customer-driven growth is possible. I summarize these here for this overview. They are then addressed in great detail, with a toolkit to provide you with actions, in Chapter seven.

1. Uniting the leadership team in communication, decision-making, and action
2. Giving permission and behaviors to model
3. Proving it with actions

MOVE FROM TALK TO ACTION

UNITE THE LEADERSHIP TEAM

How We Will Grow. How We Will Not Grow

Capacity – Culture – Competency

GIVE PERMISSION, BEHAVIORS TO MODEL

Decisions that Prove Commitment

Enable People to Deliver Value

PROVE IT WITH ACTIONS

One-Company Accountability

Congruence in Hiring, Motivation, Recognition

Behavior 1: Unite the Leadership Team

United leadership team prioritization, messaging, and partnerships need to be seen and experienced by employees so they can model this behavior with their own peers. The leadership team must be united in how they, support and enable people to deliver value, so the company can earn the right to customer-driven growth.

When I realized that a big part of my role as a customer leadership executive was to bring the leadership team together to debate and come to agreement on united actions and behaviors, it was a watershed moment.

As the role of the CCO has matured along with the importance of delivering a one-company experience, greater clarity exists among leaders on the importance of uniting. Some of our hardest work is in facilitating alignment. But without it, we experience what I call "situational commitment." During meetings when customer conversations are held, there is agreement. But when the meeting disbands, every leader translates, interprets, and communicates inconsistently back to their own departments.

As you may have experienced, silo-by-silo, leaders have their own assessment of how the company is doing, based on their own responsibilities. But leaders have not united to understand the span of work to be addressed in understanding the entire experience so that they can identify and prioritize investments. Customer experience efforts should begin by engaging and aligning leaders to understand the actions, resources and commitment necessary.

Yet this hard work often does not occur. It is passed over for the push to drive (fast) tactical actions. This push to move swiftly to tactics, although well intended, nearly always limits success. Sorting through leaders' translation of the work, and their role and required actions is hard but necessary work to be done in advance of pushing the "go" button.

Behavior 2: Give Permission and Behaviors to Model

Employees, customers, and partners need proof that your actions match your words. **With every decision you make, employees and customers are watching.** Did products get released prior to being ready because sales targets needed to be met? Were customer promises met that your partners were not prepared to deliver? Is your frontline penned in by crazy rules that prevent them from giving customers what they need, causing more cost in the end due to permissions and cycles necessary to make things right for the customer?

Killing Stupid Rules in Business-to-Business With "The Virtual Wallet"
Gavan Duff
Chief Customer Officer
MSA – The Safety Company

Gavan Duff is Chief Customer Officer for MSA, The Safety Company, where he leads their global strategy and implementation for customer experience transformation. MSA is the world's leading manufacturer of safety products designed to protect people throughout the world.

In our business-to-business operation our field-force and back-office folks are regularly navigating our processes, policies, and rules. To try to abolish many of the constraining rules that our people had to conform to regarding what they could and could not do for customers, we created the "Virtual Wallet."

This lets our employees make a decision using their own judgment about the situation and the customer they are working with. For example, they can use their virtual wallet to drop a freight charge, or accelerate shipping time for an order, or provide additional samples to a channel partner. We used to require approvals for all of these examples. We had an approval process every time we sent out a sample. It all got in the way of productivity, good decisions, and growth.

With the virtual wallet, now someone working with a client has flexibility to serve. For example, let's say they have a customer who needs

(continued)

(continued)

15 safety helmets right away. In the past, this was hard to get out for a customer. But now we give the front-line a $500 cap on a consumable item. So they can swiftly give their client those 15 safety helmets right away—especially when the client says that they are the samples for an order of 200 they will place in the future. Now they can make that decision without approval and serve the customer and save the sale.

Getting rid of all of these approvals with the simplicity of the "virtual wallet" is creating efficiency and effectiveness for our front-line, boosting their morale, and making it easier to do business with us, which is what matters with business-to-business channel partners. Speed & Agility, and Innovation & Change are core values at MSA; values that matter in these partnerships. And we are tearing down the things that get in the way … starting with some of our own rules. Acting with Speed and Agility is a growth engine for us.

People will model the example you set by your decisions. You need to *give them permission* with good examples to follow. I call this "marketing hope." There's a deliberateness that leaders must learn to take in decision-making. It's making good decisions and marketing them, which will give your transformation life. People inside your organization will be looking to your leaders to see if their language and personal behaviors have changed.

Behavior 3: Prove It with Actions. Establish One-Company Accountability

The Achilles' heel of this work is how customer issues and problems are often tossed out to a silo. Or silos individually dissect survey results and take actions. A month or two later, a report out is done on how the problem has been solved. But accountability for improving the complete experience or the business growth of the customer or client is often spotty and inconsistent.

There is a galvanizing action you can take that helps to get you out of the fray of the silo-by-silo projects and report-outs.

And that is to unite leaders for regular and customer experience accountability. We get great traction with many clients by holding what we call a "Customer Room." Convened monthly and quarterly and prior to annual planning, The customer room unites leaders to understand customers' lives, their journey with your company, and emerging issues that require focus.

This works, because rather than the CCO dissecting information, making decisions, and presenting to leaders to sell them priorities to work on, leaders make the decisions as a team. In the customer room, the outcomes of the competencies are presented by stage of the experience. Content is constantly refreshed with multiple sources of customer listening, trending of information, videos, and examples of experiences. This moves "customer centric" activities from the once-per-year energy expended when the survey results come out, to recurring focus by a united leadership team to improving customers' lives and driving growth.

And most important, in the customer room, leaders together pick the priorities. Together they identify their team members who will participate. Together they require monthly accountability from these teams in subsequent customer rooms. Like the power core examination and customer asset metrics, the customer room has been embraced throughout the world. Building a customer room to drive monthly, quarterly, and annual accountability is one of the secret weapons that we use to align leaders and drive united prioritization and action.

See the chapter on competency five for more details on specific actions for each of these categories of leadership behavior and actions. Here, I'll provide workouts we do to align and unite leaders, give permission to act, and prove it with actions. You'll also find specifics on behaviors successful leadership teams strive to practice together to build-out their customer-driven growth engine.

ACTION LAB   ORGANIZATION READINESS

A key consideration as you work to engage the leadership team is organizational readiness. We find that it is very important to have an open conversation with the C-Suite to address what has driven priorities, work, and investments in the past. For example if you are a product-driven company, process, financial metrics, and rewards center on product development and fulfillment. Here is a simple worksheet you can use to drive these conversations. The four categories—culture, process, financial reporting, and metrics and legacy practices—are the topics we find are the most critical to get on the table for discussion. Openly discussing the enablers and inhibitors as a leadership team is critical to ensuring that all issues are on the table, and everyone is ready to move forward.

Organizational Readiness: Enablers and Inhibitors to Customer-Driven Grown			
Culture	Process	Financial / Metrics	Legacy Practices

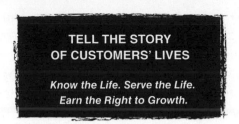

TELL THE STORY
OF CUSTOMERS' LIVES

Know the Life. Serve the Life.
Earn the Right to Growth.

What I loved about the economic downturn (okay, hang in here with me) is that it made the best companies better. In both business-to-business companies and business-to-consumer companies, the most outside-in organizations took actions that said to customers, "We know your life, we know what you're going through, and here's what we are doing as a result." Their customers took notice. And even if they didn't have money in their pockets at that moment, when they did, the magnetic pull of those gestures brought customers back. They went back to the companies that served their lives.

When I updated my book that focuses on customer and employee culture, *I Love You More than My Dog: Five Decisions that Drive Extreme Customer Loyalty in Good Times and Bad*, for the paperback edition, a big part of that revision was getting a pulse on how they fared through the worst of the economic downturn. The news was fantastic! The Container Store was thriving, IKEA found ways to bring in people with creative ways to spruce up a house in the downturn, Umpqua Bank thrived in the banking industry because they focused on being a community center, not only a bank. Business-to-business innovation giant W.L.Gore remained on their upward trajectory. These are just a few examples. Nearly everyone had either stayed in good shape or grown because these companies grow with their customers' lives at the center of how they choose to grow.

Your job is to be the company storyteller of your customers' lives. That means beginning to embed a new way of talking about the business—by leading conversations around the customer journey, their lives with you. We get so wrapped up in our projects and work that the customer is there, *but not there*. You know what I mean. We need to take the customer off spreadsheets and project plan documents, by moving this work from project plan movement to customer life improvement.

This is one of those cases where it's too hard to see how simple this can be. Think about the monthly leadership meetings you sit in today. It's probably likely that you go around the room and report out projects by silo lead and their progress in each project. By shifting that report out to accountability to stages of the customer journey, you can start to make progress.

Use Your Journey Map to Focus on Customer Priorities

Your journey map provides rigor for understanding and focusing on priorities within customer lives. It provides the map for leadership communication and accountability. Every leader I have worked with and every leadership team I have coached ask for language in a simple manner to help them galvanize the organization around this work. The customer journey provides that talk track.

By telling stories of experiences that occur to customers across journey stages, you can personalize customers' lives so that leaders and your organization care about the people behind the scores and the metrics and the data.

Focusing Our Efforts and Investments

Carol Pudnos
Head of Global Patient Experience, AbbVie
Previously Vice President of Customer Experience at Dow Corning

Carol Pudnos is Head of Global Patient Experience at AbbVie, a global biopharmaceutical company. Her role is to bring the customer journey to life inside the enterprise, educating employees and transforming the culture, engaging all stakeholders to deliver excellent customer experiences. She was previously Vice President of Customer Experience at Dow Corning Corporation.

At Dow Corning, we built a *very simple* Customer Journey Map. We organized the journey as steps that we mapped out at a very high and intuitive level. The point was to simply paint the picture from the customer's point of view. We knew this was working because within a few months, people were challenging themselves on whether the organization was delivering on the steps, but not challenging the credibility of the steps. That was good—it meant they were actually internalizing this guidance on how to look at the business.

Simplicity was the key to making this stick for us. We saw so many people going nuts with large complex maps in other places, and it was overwhelming. With our simple steps it started building the language for people right away. We started hearing people talking about their work by where it fit in those steps. It gave people the framing to change their thinking and talk.

The hard part for us came in prioritizing. We identified the risky moments, where if we didn't deliver, we would lose customer confidence. We identified these with intensive customer research and understanding approaches. We interviewed customers, just listened and heard them talk about their day and their product development decisions. We tried to understand *their* make-or-break moments in their product development cycle where we intersected with them. Then we translated all that into a short list of moments that matter.

This led us to put together a measurement framework—it was built around the make or break inflection points. We identified the tangible things we could measure and the quality of those moments, and we also measured the perception at those inflection moments.

From our make or break customer pain points or inflection points, we put together a series of questions that we wanted to know for each. We put the survey together but we never launched it as a survey. Instead, we put it in the hands of the sales professionals and gave it to them, telling them, "This is your 'discussion' framework. Now go have a discussion with your customer." We opened up a whole new way of engaging with customers with that discussion guide.

The Five Competencies Unfold to Tell the Story of Your Customers' Lives

The power of these five customer leadership competencies is that they connect in a deliberate fashion to tell the story of customers' experience with you.

- **Competency One: Honor and Manage Customers as Assets** tells you the simple metric of success: the outcome of the experience, which is how the customer asset grew or diminished.

- **Competency Two: Align around Experience** gives you a framework for leadership accountability and one-company collaboration as you align to the journey of the customer versus down the silos.

- **Competency Three: Build a Customer Listening Path** establishes a one-company approach for assembling listening, feedback, and understanding to tell the story of customers' lives and engage the organization experientially in their experiences.

- **Competency Four: Proactive Experience Reliability and Innovation** moves you from reactive silo-based cherry picking of projects to embedding skills for improving experience reliability by stage of the experience, uniting actions to imagine and improve complete customer experiences, rather than independently driven silo-based actions.

- **Competency Five: Leadership, Accountability, and Culture** unites leaders in one-company behaviors and actions to enable the competencies to become embedded into the work of the business and to enable people to act. With regular accountability, it removes what I consider the "Achilles' heel of Customer Experience"—the lack of regular accountability for experience or the change in leadership behaviors and actions.

As you build the engine of these five competencies, your role as the customer leadership executive is to connect them to be the storyteller. Tell the story of how your experience impacted customer's lives and how their reactions impact growth. Then build out of each of the five competencies, customized to your organization, to elevate the work past red-yellow-green projects to deliberately taking one-company actions to earn the right to growth.

Here is how you will eventually be able to knit together the five competencies to tell the story of your customers' life to drive united leadership engagement and company wide action:

Competency One: Honor and Manage Customers as Assets

"As a result of the experience we delivered to customers this past month or quarter or year, here's how they 'voted with their feet' to tell us if we delivered value and a one-company experience. Here is the volume and value of incoming customers, and the volume and value of lost customers, and other patterns of customer behavior that show more engagement or diminishment of the relationship. We have called and communicated with lost customers and here is the 'WHY' behind their departures."

Competency Two: Align around Experience

"Now let's traverse across the customer journey so we can understand where we impacted growth or diminishment of the customer asset. In each stage of the customer journey, where did we earn or lose the right to customer growth? Did we deliver at the priority moments along the journey?"

Competency Three: Build a Customer Listening Path

"Stage by stage of the customer journey, we will now experience what our customer has experienced in real time this past month or quarter or year. In stage 1, here are the issues emerging from the "unaided" or voluntary feedback customers gave us as they were interacting with us through our call centers, website, stores.
In stage 2 ... social media is spiking as we are not meeting requests for information. Let me play you a call-center from a customer speaking on our lack of responsiveness. In stage 3, our contract language and terms are causing a spike in customer issues. Here's a copy of that contract. As you'll see one-third of our lowest survey scores validate customer confusion with their contract experience. These survey results validate the real-time issues we are seeing as trends."

Competency Four: Proactive Experience Reliability and Innovation

"Now we will identify our performance operationally in the priority touchpoints with customers across their journey with us. In stage two, as customers are reaching out to get information about our products as they do their research, the three operational metrics most critical to the customer experience are not meeting our minimum acceptable performance standard. It's no wonder complaints are spiking. Here is where we are interrupting customers' ability to get value from our experience.

We also see in stage 3 that we are below our standard performance for the cycle of getting a proposal to the customer. Before this turns into an issue for our clients, let's get a team on this situation."

Competency Five: Leadership, Accountability, and Culture

"Customers walking into our bank are encountering three legacy rules, which are causing the majority of the complaints and causing more than 50 percent of transactions to require a manager's involvement. We need to remove these inhibiting rules and let our employees and customers know."

Monthly: Ok, let's identify as a leadership team, which top three opportunities we are going to build a team on. And now let's have the current teams show us the progress they are making on their efforts.

Before annual planning: We've stepped through our customers' experience with us as part of annual planning, and we now have the top five company-wide priorities for next year to focus on to earn greater growth through our customer assets."

IMPROVE THE
BUSINESS ENGINE

*Simplify Prioritization,
Accountability, and Annual
Planning.*

While you have the CCO role, you may not realize you also need to "earn" the right to people's engagement in the work. What we've learned with every client is that to earn the engagement from leaders, you must show how building the five-competency customer-driven growth engine simplifies and improves the processes of running the business.

When the five competencies are embedded into the organization with leadership behavior, they are so clear that they become *the work* of the organization. There is no separation between the "customer" work and the "real" work. They connect to growth, and they shift attitudes from chasing the score to caring about and improving customer lives.

You're probably not there yet.

Within most organizations, there is a process for the following areas listed below. You may have more, but these are the key understood processes:

- Product/Service Planning and Development
- Sales Planning and Achievement
- IT Planning and Implementation
- Corporate-wide Annual Planning and Investments

The degree to which these major planning and implementation areas of your company integrate with one another varies by organization, industry, and leadership. But the common denominator for most is: the customer work gets layered on top of the "real" work.

For this work to be sustainable and drive long-term transformation, it needs to become a company-unifying framework.

You need to be clear with your leaders that the five competencies take reactivity, duplication, and overspending out of the operation.

You can use the five competencies to establish appreciation for working as a united leadership team to remove reactivity (to squeaky-wheel issues, one-off customer breakdowns, and executive customer fire-drills) in a very deliberate way. Most important, it will help you to engage leaders in united decision-making to improve the four big culprits that cause this work to stall: silo-based prioritization and investment, capacity creation, holding people accountable, and annual planning.

Culprit 1: Silo-based Prioritization and Investment

Current Prioritization: In general, silo-based operations are not working in line of sight to one another to build complete end-to-end customer experiences. Silos often go separately to the (well-intended) survey dashboard where they dissect data question by question (rather than by customer journey). Here silos individually cherry-pick projects and priorities by driving actions they believe will drive "lift" on survey question scores that can be attributable back to them. This drives the prioritization of many projects all coming from different silo-based points of view. All these projects give a false positive that customers' interests and needs are being focused on. Projects overlap, as they are often assembled with silo-based prioritization.

Future Prioritization takes a one-company approach as leaders traverse the customer journey on a monthly, quarterly, and annual basis to select the few impactful priorities versus the many silo-based priorities. Customer listening and operational process information are assembled across the customer journey to provide an updated and regular view of emerging priorities. This informs leaders of the key strategic priorities they must unite on improve.

Culprit 2: Work Is Layered On and Capacity Creation Is Not Addressed

Currently, in most organizations, when new cross-functional teams are assembled to react to squeaky-wheel customer issues, these teams tax already busy people. And these reactively assembled projects feel layered onto the "real" work of participants. Fatigue, exhaustion, and feelings of "Why are we doing this?" ensue.

Intelligent capacity creation is an important benefit of building out this engine with leaders. Every time I meet with a client, I ask how good they are at building their "stop doing" list. That question is almost always greeted with laughter. And here's why. There's no common framework for deciding what starts and what stops. It becomes a lobbying effort for projects, driven by subjective decision-making based on who does the best "sell" of why the project should stay or go.

As a first step in this work, one of the things we do is line up projects under the stages of the experience. All projects from all silos get lined up. This gives visibility to duplicate actions and capacity drain. Moving forward, the disciplined process for accountability with leaders that comes out of the customer room process in competency five establishes a protocol for making trade-offs in a united manner. Leaders decide together what projects stay and what go. What is most important to drive customer growth?

Culprit 3: Lack of Rigor in Holding People Accountable

Current accountability to customer-driven priorities in your company might sound like this: "Billing survey scores are low. Jim, you run billing, take a look and then report back to us what needs to be fixed." Sound familiar? Jim takes a well-intended look at the processes to see what is out of alignment from his team's point of view. They work on a few things. In the next meeting, Jim reports out that they've taken care of their issues.

Here's what's challenging with that approach. First, fixing "billing" from the billing department standpoint does not necessarily elevate or improve the entire billing experience. The experience can be disappointing for a host of reasons. Maybe the billing cycle was not explained clearly to customers so there is misunderstanding. Maybe the terms on the form have too much jargon (which may not look like jargon to the well-meaning billing team), and the list goes on. Second, the old-fashioned report at the executive weekly meeting pushes the work back to project plans with red-yellow-green dots. The emphasis is on "did you get it done?" rather than "how did you improve the lives of our customers?"

Squeaky-wheel issues lobbed to operational areas or cross-functional teams to "take a look" are inconsistent in rigor and process. What success should look like is not clearly understood or agreed upon. When the silos work on something from their area, success may be the reduction of an inside-out metric. In general, there is not a regularly understood set of actions and outcomes when "take a look at it" is requested. And more to the point, the "take a look at it" cycle by its very nature is reactive.

Future accountability with the five-competency engine occurs because through its process, leaders agree in unison what the focus should be. That is a result of the rigor that comes from building a customer room (see competency five). The information and storytelling of customers' lives assembled from competencies three and four point to priorities. Then leaders agree in unison what resources each will contribute to investigate and improve the complete customer experience.

Teams assembled by the entire leadership team, are tasked to deliver a monthly set of predetermined action items until they are implementing a solution. They are guided to diagnose problems and propose customer-centric solutions by a professional customer experience facilitator. When a solution takes hold and customer complaints on the issue start to decline (which cannot be "gamed" to get a better result), the teams can be rewarded—based on improving customers' lives.

Growing Pains: Passion Meets Reality!

Chris Dawson
*Vice President & General Manager, Global Sales
and Consumer Experience Division
BRP – Bombardier Recreational Products*

Chris Dawson is Vice President and General Manager, Consumer Experience and Global Sales Division, of BRP, Bombardier Recreational Products, where he leads global consumer experience, sales management, go-to market activities, network development, after-sales service, parts, accessories, and clothing for Ski-Doo, Lynx, Can-Am, and Sea-Doo brands, and Evinrude in International markets.

In any major change initiative, a key ingredient is the desire to change, and certainly in that regard we had no lack of passion! However, despite our efforts to remain focused, many small projects and initiatives sprouted within the company, each justified with the need to enhance the customer experience. While many of these had merit, the lack of focus on a few key (and high ROI) initiatives meant we did not maintain the momentum that we started with.

Suddenly our progress felt less tangible, and a lot of employees were asking, "Where is this going?" So we have reorganized our efforts, achieved alignment across the management team, and assigned leadership to a specific executive. Now, it is not enough to simply state that a project will "enhance the customer experience." People now need to justify that this is the best use of our limited resources, and that it has a high ROI. As a result, we have stopped almost all of the smaller initiatives in favor of concerted efforts around two priority "moments of truth." We need more wins, both for the benefit of our employees and for our dealers (and ultimately for our customers!).

Naturally there was some concern that this approach was limiting, and I'm sure there are still some people who are harboring frustrations that we are not doing enough to satisfy each customer. To quell the concerns we have been communicating more with our employees:

- We need to focus; we are doing too much
- The truth is that duplicate efforts are costly and impede action

(continued)

(*continued*)

- Management is united in this approach
- We need to focus on the best ROI initiatives for revenue potential and cost savings

By talking it through, we have reached broad agreement that this is the way to go, that by being more focused and cohesive around the world we will achieve more. We are just kicking off our renewed efforts, but so far, so good—and the passion remains.

Culprit 4: Annual Planning and IT Investment

Current annual planning is largely a silo-by-silo endeavor, because there is not a consistent framework to drive rigor in prioritization and planning. Planning starts with each silo's budget allocated, existing projects, and their scorecards. Customer experience priorities are established separately by silo, as a result of the unco-ordinated plans built by each. Annual planning is the Achilles' heel of delivering a one-company customer experience for this reason.

Future annual planning starts with the framework of the customer journey. The customer room meeting that is held with all leadership before annual planning trends and accumulates the year's information to unite and inform leaders of focus and priorities. Leaders debate and agree and decisions are made which comprehensively connect product, sales, IT, customer experience, service priorities. Then the money is doled back out to the silos to plan. Line of sight changes everything.

Summary

Many factors related to leadership and culture will impact your ability to achieve role clarity, united leadership engagement, and successfully implement the five competencies.

While the five Customer Leadership Competencies frame the work to be done in your role as CCO, it is attitudinal shifts in leadership thinking and behaviors and your engagement to unite leaders that will determine the successful transformation of your business.

These are the cornerstones to a successful transformation of your business and engagement of your leadership team in enabling change. Refer back to them frequently as you begin to build out your more tactical plans for implementing the five competencies. They will serve you well.

- **Focus on Growth and Customers as Assets**. *Remove Survey Score Addiction.*
- **Identify Your Power Core**. *Know What Helps or Hinders the Work.*
- **Unite Leadership and Connect Talk to Action**. *Eliminate the "Baloney" Factor.*
- **Tell the Story of Customers' Lives**. *Care Why Customers Stay or Go.*
- **Improve the Business Engine**. *Earn the Right to do This Work.*

ACTION LAB LEADERSHIP TEAM INVOLVEMENT

Sound an alarm if you present this five-competency approach or other strategy and receive this response, "Sounds great, go ahead." That's a trap. Rinse and repeat. This is in fact the traditional way in which leaders advocate for this work. Agreement is made and the work falls on the CCO and team and sometimes "loyalty leads" to go off and try to do the work. After that, leadership team interaction is "situational." When survey results are presented or issues identified, conversations occur.

(continued)

(*continued*)

But that does not unite the leadership team into action or embed behaviors that they take back to their teams.

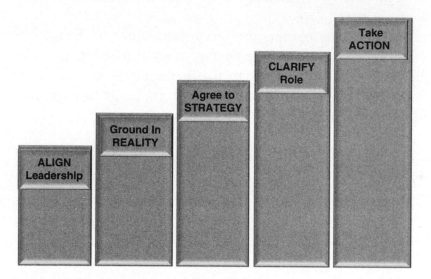

Stair-Stepping Leadership Engagement

1. **Align the Leadership Team.** Establish alignment and leadership team understanding of what customer experience is. Get beyond the "shiny object" syndrome with specifics. Clarify how customer experience is not customer service. Explicitly gain agreement of leadership team involvement.

2. **Ground in Reality.** Step leaders through the current experience of a priority customer journey to have a firsthand view of what is being delivered as a result of the silos working independently. Rate the current one-company experience reliability in each journey stage.

3. **Agree to Strategy.** Translate the work to the specific actions and tactics that will lead you to achieve your strategy for customer-driven growth. With the five competencies in this book, I provide you with specific actions that you can propose and discuss with leaders. We find

that without this level of specificity, the work remains conceptual, and it's hard to get past the hand-wave. With the five competencies, we work with leaders to build the engine that recycles—and show explicitly how they have a role in building and sustaining it.

4. **Clarify the CCO Role.** Use the specificity of the actions that you outline as a way to establish role clarity for the customer leadership executive role. Gain agreement with your C-Suite that the CCO role is to actively work with the leadership team to architect the customer-driven growth engine. The role is to build and facilitate the build of the engine that unites leaders in decision-making, accountability, and action.

5. **Take Action with the Leadership Team.** Now that you have done the groundwork, you should be in a position to move forward. Review the five competencies and determine where you stand today. Gain further commitment after this higher level of understanding that they still want to move forward building your customer-driven growth engine. Begin to build out and take actions. See each competency chapter for first actions to begin executing on with the leadership team.

Engaging Leaders in the 5 Competencies

Mark Slatin
Senior Vice President – Client Experience Manager
Sandy Spring Bank

Mark Slatin is Senior Vice President and Client Experience Manager at Sandy Spring Bank, where he leads the client experience effort to drive sustainable growth across all business units. With $4.4 billion in assets, Sandy Spring Bank provides comprehensive financial solutions to clients across Maryland and Northern Virginia.

(continued)

(continued)

Taking on a leadership role in improving our client experience required the backing of our CEO, Dan Schrider. I had his support when I stepped into the role. I then set out to establish relationships with the entire leadership team, to engage them in this work.

One of the first things we did was build our Client Experience Leadership Council. Comprised of senior leaders in critical positions throughout the bank, they run all the diverse business units that drive our clients' experiences. To make this work stick and transformative, they had to have an ownership stake.

I recognize the importance of building relationships with our executives and council members and have spent time getting to know them, to learn who they are and what makes them tick. Everyone on the team has a heart for client experience and yet negotiates a balance with their day job. We aspire to have client experience and our day jobs not be seen as two different things.

With the council, we first agreed on the five competencies approach set forth in this book. Next, we set up five distinct teams, one for each competency. Each team has an executive sponsor who rolls up his or her sleeves alongside the other senior leaders, who meet every other week to shape our strategy and make important decisions. Every quarter, we hold a Client Experience Executive meeting with the entire senior leadership team. This engages them each step of the way, building momentum across the organization.

As a result of this approach, this leadership team has guided the outcome and customization of each of the five competencies. I have played the role of the enabler, and of the "glue"—linking it all together so the work can move forward.

We are now embedding this work into the cycle of how we plan and invest. In fact, we have made a significant commitment to client experience in establishing our annual Customer Experience (CX) planning retreat. The entire executive team and CX Leadership Council went offsite for two full days to connect, reflect, and plan together. It built unity and consistency and helped us to tackle the challenges that are natural with this work. More hands together pushing that rock up the hill has been a successful formula for us. The fact that these hands all impact the business operation puts the accountability on all of us to keep pushing to make this part of how we collectively run the bank.

3

Competency One: Honor and Manage Customers as Assets

HONOR AND MANAGE CUSTOMERS AS ASSETS.

Know the Growth and Loss of Customers and Care About "WHY?"

"Experience" Accountability =

Customers as Assets:

Align leaders to make a defining performance metric – the growth or loss of your customer base. Shift to a simple understanding of customer-driven growth success.

- Growth of Customers
- Loss of Customers
- Business Growth

New Customers, Volume and Value.

Lost Customers, Volume and Value? WHY?

Definition: Honor and Manage Customers as Assets

This is the clincher competency. It is what makes this work legitimate. It's why you are in business: to grow the customer asset.

With this competency, the purpose is to shift to a simple understanding and measurement of success when a company achieves customer-driven growth. Customer asset metrics track *what customers actually did* versus translating (and debating) what they *say they might do* via survey results. No regression analysis by survey question or debating results required. The company either grew the customer asset as a result of the experience delivered, or it did not. As leaders learn and embrace these simple metrics that measure success, their demand for improvement will rival their demand for meeting sales goals and revenue targets.

Leaders must start taking it personally that customers are departing from their business. They need to care about the "math" between customers in and customers out—because that delta drives growth. They need to make the connection between customer experience improvement and the movement of these metrics. Customer asset metrics create a way for executives to know and care about the shifting behavior within your customer base, which indicates if your bond with your customers is growing or shrinking.

Making a defining performance metric of customer experience, the growth or loss of the customer base can be explained easily to the board. Importantly, it gives your executives a platform from which they can personally talk about this work and take ownership of it, as it connects to business growth.

Defining What Success Looks Like

Tom Botts
Executive Vice President & Chief Customer Officer
Denihan Hospitality Group

Tom Botts is Executive Vice President and Chief Customer Officer at Denihan Hospitality Group, responsible for developing and executing a holistic approach to customer experience across brands and properties. Denihan Hospitality group is a full-service hotel management and development company that owns and/or operates boutique hotels in major urban markets in the United States.

One of the things we have really focused on is getting the metrics correct so we all know what success looks like; that we are all marching in the same direction. Once we got started, we found out quickly that even the wording, or the lexicon of getting terms aligned was necessary. And that has been more difficult than we thought it would be. You say potato, I say potato!

So, we've spent a lot of time defining and getting our terms, our measurements, and our data for reporting in alignment. The first thing we did was to focus on how we define how we interact with our customers, and how we measure that interaction. We immediately discovered there was inconsistency in what people considered channels in how performance was reported; therefore, revenue by channel had inconsistent definitions.

Another focus has been getting straight two terms in the hotel industry: *booking* and *consuming*, and how we report that from property to property, and through booking engines. There is a time when people are *booking* reservations and a time when they are *consuming* them. Booking is a forward-looking indicator. Consuming is what actually happened in the previous period. These were reported in varied and inconsistent ways.

We needed to get the baselines of those standards and definitions down in 2014. And that's what we did. It was our blocking and tackling year to get the actual definitions right and build the baseline systems and technology so everything rolls up consistently. This year is about optimizing and rationalizing the brands and the platforms we invested in. And it's about re-engaging. We thought we had understanding as we had a lot of heads nodding in agreement, but we have work to do to go back and realign the organization from individual silo work to delivering an end-to-end experience.

These customer asset metrics build passion across the organization and establish a simple rallying cry for leaders. They are tracked by all of my clients, with the conversations going something like this: *Rather than talking about customer retention, let's begin each meeting discussing our raw numbers of*:

- Number of new customers earned in this period, by volume and value (power of your acquisition engine); sorted by segment.

- Number of lost or lapsed customers lost in this period, by volume and value (power of the experience and value perceived); how many increased their purchases, and how many declined in their level of engagement with you? Sorted by segment.
- Behavioral patterns that show increase or weakening of the customer relationships.
- Movement of customers within value segments.
- Referrals from existing customers.

It is important to present your Customer asset metrics in whole numbers of customers, not retention rates, so that there is a clear connection between people and the math. For example, we brought in 22,000 customers, but we lost 27,000 customers. That is much more powerful (and personal) than "Our retention rate is x percent." We give ourselves a false positive when just retention rates are reported because they don't glaringly show the number of people who left—who deliberately stopped doing business or lapsed or reduced their business connection.

Yet, when I ask executives if they know the volume and value of their new customers and compare it monthly, weekly, and annually to the volume and value of lost customers, it's not top of mind. "It's in our data" is often the answer, but it's buried. Silos own their portion of the information, such as sales performance or marketing performance, but a one-company articulation of the growth or loss of the customer base has usually not been established or tracked.

As a result, the opportunity to galvanize the organization around a simple ROI metric of customer experience impact is lost. Customer asset growth or loss is not brought up in a fearless way at every key meeting with employees and customers. The true measure of whether customers found value from their experience and treatment is not actively discussed, debated, or factored into decisions, strategy, and action.

Baseline Customer Asset Metrics

Customer asset metrics have five basic components that establish simple metrics connected to customer-driven growth. You will need to customize these components to your business model, and we find that the activity of leaders working together to define your version of them is both eye-opening and accelerates the work. The simplicity of this "customer math" is what makes this a powerful tool for you to gain the attention of leadership and connect the work to growth. An Action Lab in this chapter provides a tool to begin to determine your version of customer asset metrics.

These baseline customer asset metrics give your leadership five simple things to care about regarding customer-driven growth.

Customer Asset Metric 1: New Customers—Volume and Value

It's likely that your marketing and/or sales organizations are tracking this metric in some manner. It's also likely that they may be tracking this performance independent of one another, based on the objectives for their organization. What defines a "new" customer may also have multiple definitions within your data. Companies still tend to be acquisition companies, so new customers will be relatively easy to track and trend. The work is to unite the definitions and databases so that you can achieve a company-wide rolled-up number of new customers.

What is more difficult to track is the *quality or value* of incoming customers. One incoming customer is usually not equal to one exiting customer. This one-for-one approach gives a false positive, especially when only retention rates are tracked. You may be holding steady at a 73 percent retention rate, but the quality of customers exiting is usually of much higher value than newly acquired customers. And, by tracking the rate and not whole numbers of customers arriving and departing, leaders also miss the power of knowing and taking it personally that x thousands of customers left you. This numeric reality of whole numbers is very powerful. So you've got to track and measure two things:

- How many new customers did you acquire in the period?
- What is their projected value?

Customer Asset Metric 2: Lost Customers—Volume and Value and Reasons Why

The volume and value of lost customers need to be paired with new customer information to establish true customer asset growth for your company. This is about math and about uniting definitions and data so that you can establish a one-company way to identify and measure lost or lapsed customers. I have recently added lapsed customers to this metric because you should want to know about customers who have not returned within a period of time, in addition to those customers who have stopped interacting with you entirely.

In addition to knowing which customers have left, you need to know the reasons *why* they left. Without knowing or caring about this, the organization misses the opportunity to galvanize people into taking action. You have to create a purposeful way to enable customers to inform you they're cutting you loose. And you need to care enough about the potency of this information to find a way to collect their feedback.

You will also have to determine how to connect with your exiting customers to find out the "why" behind their departure. We find that reaching out to lost customers, when done in a genuine manner to honestly find out what happened, can even earn the right to a customer return. As part of this process you'll need a method to track and understand the following:

- How many new customers were lost or lapsed?
- What is their value?
- Who are they?
- Why did they leave?

Think of your own experiences as a customer. When you end a relationship with a business, and never hear from them again, doesn't this confirm that your business didn't mean that much to them?

How We Track & Reward Customer Growth

Misha Logvinov
Chief Customer Officer
Lithium Technologies

Misha Logvinov is Chief Customer Officer at Lithium Technologies. Misha is responsible for leading Lithium's strategic programs to ensure long-term customer success, and enhancing and solidifying Lithium's customer-centric culture by orchestrating the entire customer value chain across functions and geographies.

We know that 70 percent of our revenue comes from current customers and 30 percent is from new customers acquisition. We are very open and transparent with the growth or loss of our customer base and the importance of the growth of this asset. We consistently talk about this at all-hands meetings, with messaging also translated into internal department and group meetings. It's a very active topic for us.

We have evolved over time in how we track the growth or shrinkage of our customer relationships, as our ability to look at behavioral data and data connected to product usage. What we are tracking now continues to frame our conversations so that people care not only about the retention numbers but also about the behaviors of customers that we need to focus on. Currently we are tracking:

- Install base/net customer growth (customers gained minus customers lost, weighted for value).
- Renewing and nonrenewing customers and why.
- White space assessment—are customers using what they bought? Why or why not?
- Customer movement within value segments.

We have made everyone in the company feel the pain in the wallet when we are not good at install base growth. We have moved from

(continued)

(*continued*)

rewarding only for acquisition to net growth of the customer base: incoming minus outgoing customers. This is reflected in everyone's bonus because the end-to-end experience impacts whether a customer stays or goes and continues to invest with us. We use this information as the starting point for our annual planning.

Customer Asset Metric 3: Do the Math—Net Growth or Loss of Your Customer Asset

This is where the *clincher* part of this competency comes in. Once you build a one-company method of tracking and identifying incoming customers volume and value, and lost customers volume and value, you can simply show the outcome of the experience you delivered to customers as net customer growth or loss.

The ability to roll-up customer data in this meaningful way for many of the CEOs and boards we work with has made the connection between customer experience and growth. We get the most traction and understanding when customers gained minus customers lost is represented visually. A compelling and simple representation can show the opportunity for incremental growth that might have been achieved if more customers had stayed.

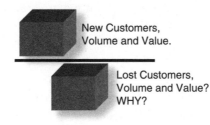

This visual story pushes leaders to care about "why?" The simplicity of this math is powerful, and whets the appetite for wanting to know more about actual customer behavior.

These first two customer asset metrics are at the highest level, the outcome of the experience you are delivering to customers—I call it "customers voting with their feet."

And I have found it very powerful to always begin meetings with this simple report card on the company's ability to earn the right to customer growth.

Customer Asset Metric 4: A Simple Set of Customer Behaviors Indicating Growth or Loss of Relationship

These are customer behaviors to help you to tell the story of how engaged customers are with you, identifying behaviors that show both increased and decreased involvement and perception of value. This adds dimension to the customer asset metrics story. Some examples of these behaviors are below. However these will need to be customized for your business.

- Volume and trend of customers using products or services purchased. This is very effective to understand potential value erosion. For example, in Software as a Service businesses (SaaS), watching and knowing this performance is valuable in both directing proactive actions with customers based on their adoption or usage, and in predicting revenue and profit. Use whole numbers, not only percentages, to make the results personal and to take customers off the spreadsheet.
- Revenue and profitability by customer group or segment (customer segment movement). Most of my clients find it very powerful to present the movement of customers shifting from one value segment to another. This is highly effective because the ability to report this performance requires a deliberate strategy and one-company agreement on customer segmentation—something that is still lacking in many organizations. When feasible, it's important to identify and discuss these clients by name so that the focus is on improving customers' lives, not numbers.
- Customers who did not renew in a subscription- or renewal-based model. Use whole numbers in addition to percentages, to humanize the information.

- Customers who lapsed or were lost after an incident. This is very powerful as it shows customer movement connected to an incident and their perception of your company's recovery.

- Referrals received by customer segment. When I bring this up, most clients' immediate response is "we can't do that." The work is to determine how to engage, encourage and acknowledge customer referrals in a genuine manner. The examined company often spends time wringing its hands over why customers aren't referring them, examining how the referral rates differ by customer group. You need to use this information to dig into the reasons behind the numbers and drive change as a result of what you learn.

My recommendation is to limit your customer asset baseline metrics to no more than five. The rest of the five competency framework will add to the story of customer experiences with more detail and granularity. Keep these metrics to the highest-level outcome-based metrics.

And the most important tip: Just get started. Don't wait until the system is automated to turn these out onto a spreadsheet. You may need to go grab the information manually as you begin. "Clunky" is okay in your early generations of customer asset metrics. Do what you can with the data that is accessible. It's likely that all the data you need won't be available in the right form. A valuable part of this work is aligning data organization and access.

Once you begin, you can course-correct over time as your data matures and become more consistent and reliable. A good database marketer is crucial here, but you must keep this person focused. Without clarity of specific deliverables, the data are so delectable that they can spend hours and hours slicing and dicing them. Keep it simple. Keep it simple. Keep it simple.

These customer asset metrics will connect your work to the growth of the business. Because they are simple, they create a way for executives to know and care about the shifting behavior within your customer base, which indicates if their bond with you is growing or shrinking.

Making Channel Partners an Asset of Our Business

Gavan Duff
Executive Director, Global Customer Loyalty
MSA – The Safety Company

Gavan Duff is Chief Customer Officer at MSA, The Safety Company, where he leads their global strategy and implementation for customer experience transformation. MSA is the world's leading manufacturer of safety products designed to protect people throughout the world.

We are a business-to-business company and we have channel partners who are very valuable to us. Yet we'd not really thought of these channel partners as assets. In a traditional B-B company fashion, we considered them a "product-selling arm." But they are our assets. Where our relationship with them goes, so goes the growth of our business.

To begin this new focus, we had to consistently define our channel partner customers, and segment them to be able to track and add value in our relationships with them. What I found was that we had all the pieces to know that information, but we didn't have consistent definitions or reporting or a one-company view of their relationships. So as a first step we determined how to track who they are and in a simple manner, the strength of the relationship.

- Which partners are new?
- Which partners have lapsed in their orders/relationship with us?
- What partners in our portfolio have we lost? Why?

More important than just knowing the growth of channel partners, we needed to be proactive about their experience. As a result we have built something we call an "Action Tracker" On a monthly basis we now

(continued)

(*continued*)

have an event that tells us how we are performing in delivering value to channel partners. This tool gives us an outside-in view so we can see how the customer views us from an ease of doing business standpoint. We now have a one-company view on:

- Cycle of events in their buying patterns
- Triggers when they are at inflection points where we need to be proactive
- Tracking of how we are doing in delivering and meeting their needs
- How we are helping to grow their businesses, not just how much we sell
- Feedback to follow up when goods are delivered

As a result, our leadership conversations are shifting. We now start with the channel partner and what we must do to earn the right to their growth. We don't (always) start with the survey score. We are very transparent with this information with our people. We trend this information, review it regularly across functions, and then we take the data and post it for people to see. It is a big part of our regular training on "What is customer experience?" We are embedding that channel partners are an asset of our business. This is changing the culture of the company, and driving a one-company view of how we contribute to channel partner growth, and how they contribute to ours.

ACTION LAB   **YOUR CUSTOMER ASSET METRICS**

Here is a worksheet to help you build your version of customer asset metrics. As noted above, keep it simple and just begin. Get started with the data you have now. It is completely normal if all data is not easily accessible or aligned across the silos. Many of my clients build their first version on an Excel spreadsheet. Most important, use this information to engage leaders and unite them in talking about the growth or loss of the customer asset as a definition of success.

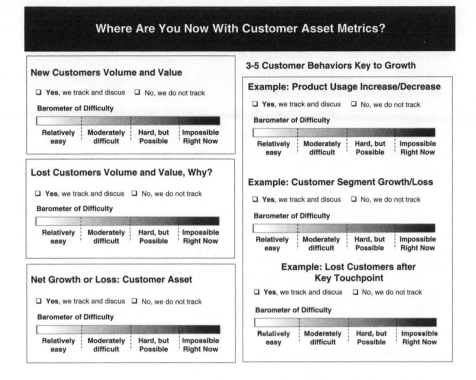

Leadership Shift Required

Leaders must start taking it personally that customers are departing from their business. They need to care about the "math" between customers in and customers out—because that delta drives growth. They need to make the connection between customer experience improvement and the movement of these metrics. Customer asset metrics create a way for executives to know and care about the shifting behavior within your customer base, which indicates if their bond with you is growing or shrinking.

Two leadership shifts are required to drive this work forward.

1. Building one-company metrics that include the growth or loss of the customer asset. Using the metrics to establish the connection of the customer experience to business growth.
2. Evolving leadership behavior to care why customers stay or leave your business.

In the previous sections, we discussed the shift away from survey score addition to measuring customers as assets. Here we will discuss the second pivotal shift required: honoring the customer asset and changing the focus to "earning the right" to growth by honoring customers.

There is a difference in the messaging of leaders who focus on earning the right to growth by improving the life of customers. And there is a difference in the company actions that follow.

When the intent of the business is to improve customers' lives, the work is to know and focus on improving the experiences that are proven to disrupt, dishonor, or deliver unreliable experiences that interrupt customers' lives.

When you improve those experiences, you add value, and customers will stay, and tell other people about you ... and, yes, the survey scores will improve. But more important than survey scores, you will earn the right to net customer asset growth—which connects directly to business growth—no regression analysis required.

See the leadership "recipe cards" at the end of this chapter to guide the adoption of customers as assets and earning the right to growth by improving customers' lives.

Competency One Impact When Implemented

For many companies, just putting together these simple articulations of "incoming or outgoing" customers or "value" requires an alignment in definition. It certainly involves alignment in data and databases as every part of the organization and every silo often have varying definitions. The power of uniting leaders to agree on this new metric is not small. In fact, we often engage the CEO and CFO and CMO in the build-out of customer asset metrics. Their participation makes it personal for them, and drives with more success, the embedding of this new metric into the business. The role of the CCO is to unite leaders in establishing your version of customer asset metrics.

Rather than talking about customer retention rates or survey scores, begin meetings throughout your company by fearlessly discussing the outcome of the experience delivered across your organization to customers. Did the customer asset grow or shrink as a result of the experience delivered?

It will take work to be able to deliver these sentences below on a monthly, quarterly, and annual basis. But when you do, you will begin a transformative leadership shift in how they view and hold people accountable for business success.

> *"As a result of the experience we delivered to customers this past month or quarter or year, this is the outcome of the growth or loss of the customer asset we earned. This number is the volume and value of incoming customers, and the volume and value of lost customers, and other patterns of customer behavior that show more engagement or diminishment of the relationship. We reached out to lost customers and we know the points in the journey where we let customers down, and they voted with their feet and departed."*

Across every industry I work with, customer asset metrics are successful in engaging executive leadership in a customer-centric transformation. They become engaged in the conversation because of the simplicity of the metrics and their connection to earning the right to growth.

Summary

The power of Competency One: Managing and Honoring Customers as Assets, is in establishing a one-company measure of customer-driven growth that is as clearly understood by leaders as sales and revenue goals. As executives learn and embrace these metrics, their demand for improvement will rival their demand for meeting those targets. Experience improvement will become a growth strategy.

Survey scores have been relied upon in many companies as the primary metric to determine the strength of the relationship with the customer. And many questions remain about the connection between the survey outcome and its connection to growth. Customer asset metrics cut through those questions. They measure what customers *did* as a result of their experience with you, not what they say they are going to do via survey results. Customer asset metrics provide the net growth or loss of your customer asset and behavioral shifts indicating growth or shrinkage of the customer relationship.

This enables survey results to be *part* of a balanced understanding of the experience delivered to your customer. Customer asset metrics will reduce the pressure on the survey as the only metric that the company focuses on and discusses, reducing the debate about survey results, the survey mechanism, and its connection to revenue and profitability.

The power of the five competencies is that they connect multiple sources of information, storytelling, leadership, and company engagement to build caring about customers' lives, from the customers' point of view. The balance of analytical, qualitative, and quantitative information presented along the customer journey gives you the proving points you need to focus resources and commitment. This makes customer experience improvement understood and appreciated with as much rigor as leaders understand sales, marketing, and financial operations and goals.

Honoring Our Customers as Assets

Nick Frunzi
Chief Customer Officer
ESRI

Nick Frunzi is Chief Customer Officer at ESRI, where he directs strategy, metrics, requirements, and resources to enhance customer retention and loyalty and create competitive advantage. ESRI is the world's largest geospatial technology provider, enabling governments, industry leaders, and many others to connect with the analytic knowledge they need to make critical decisions that shape the planet.

With our focus on honoring customers as assets, we have been on the lookout for random rules that prove otherwise. For example, we have a cloud offering that, like most, gives a certain number of credits for a customer's consumption of the technology. We had a rule programmed in that if a customer burned through their assigned credits, without a lot of advance notice or conversation, we shut down their service. This was done by a technological computer rule—when you cross that line we just shut you down. We heard some churn and had a team working on this, but no one would acknowledge how the rule was set or why!

We have now instilled a new process—and that is—before ANY customer's service gets turned off, there are conversations inside the company to discuss the situation, as well as conversations directly with the customer. Autopilot service termination has ceased. Now when a customer is out of credits we reach out with a human interaction versus an automated switch that turns the customer's service off. We've switched our focus to keeping the customer running versus random rule adherence.

The balanced approach of the five-competency framework will move this work beyond being a "leap of faith" to work connected with an outcome as equally understood and desired as sales goals, campaign outcomes, or cost reduction. Make no mistake, these goals and actions compete with this work. Customer asset metrics will help you remove the competition.

The power of competency one is that it lays the groundwork to enable the work because it connects to growth and return-on-investment. And it begins the critical culture shift among leaders for caring about the "WHY?" behind customers who stay or go.

ACTION LAB   **LEADERSHIP BEHAVIORS**

Every leader I've ever worked with has asked for explicit actions that they can take to show their commitment. I've started calling these actions "recipe cards" because to be successful, they need to be short, simple, and easy to own. To support you with Competency 1: Honor and Manage Customers as Assets, I have listed a summary of key behaviors for your C-suite, which will prove

(*continued*)

(*continued*)

commitment with united messaging and actions. Don't take these on all at once. Stair-step them. Get agreement with your leadership team. But then don't stop once you start.

Leadership Behaviors to Drive Transformation

Competency 1: Honor and Manage Customers as Assets

Align the Leadership Team	Give Permission
United Messaging: Focus on Customer Asset Growth	**Enable People to Grow The Customer Asset**
Every leader starts their meetings with employees by fearlessly sharing the growth or loss of the Customer Asset.	Create a "Kill a Stupid Rule" movement, encouraging employees to identify rules that erode customer trust and diminish employee's ability to do their job.
Evolve leadership messaging from "getting the score" to "earning the right" to customer growth.	Reward for the identification of rules that just don't make sense. And kill those rules! Let employees know. (market hope)

Prove It with Action

Put the Voice of the Customer In Your Ear.

Every month, call lost customers to care about the "why" and humanize the life of the customer. Tell the story of customers' lives to your employees.

Reward for Customer Asset Growth.

Move your overall "customer focus" success metric from survey scores to overall performance in customer asset growth. The true measure of your Customer experience.

Competency Two: Align around Experience

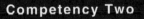

Competency Two

ALIGN AROUND EXPERIENCE.

Give Leaders a Framework for Guiding the Work of the Organization.
Unite Accountability as Customers Experience You. Not Down Your Silos.

"Experience" Accountability –

Awareness & Research	Assess & Sample	Develop Solution	Partner & Contract	Service & Support	Strategic Partnership

#2 *Align Around Experience*:

Align the Operation Around Customer Experience Delivery & Innovation. "Earn the Right" to Customer Asset Growth.
- Customer Journey
- Focus on Priorities
- Leadership Language

Definition: Alignment around Experience

Companies that transform how they grow and are deliberate about it, do so because they think about the people at the end of their decisions. The intent of their work is to "earn the right" to growth by improving customers' lives. A journey framework, even in its simplest form, when used with consistency provides rigor to understand where the priorities in customers' lives are. By using the journey to look comprehensively across what the company delivers, it enables leadership to make choices. This moves the work from "boiling the ocean," trying to map and drive improvement on all the touchpoints (Visio blindness, anyone?) to *focusing* on those that matter most in the lives of customers.

That is the *real* transformational power in building a customer (and employee) journey map. It is to embed a new starting point for the work of the organization. Instead of starting with the silos, **the customer journey gives you a framework to begin with your customers' lives.**

This establishes a framework for leaders to use to guide the direction of the business and drive accountability. It enables them to hold people accountable for improving customers' lives and uniting independent silo scorecards. Every leader I have worked with and every leadership team I have coached have asked for simple language to galvanize people around customer-driven growth. The customer journey provides that talk track.

FIRST JOURNEY MAP EVER For The Smithsonian

Samir Bitar
Director of the Office of Visitor Services
Smithsonian Institution

Samir Bitar is Director of the Office of Visitor Services at the Smithsonian Institution, where he is responsible for developing and overseeing the implementation of the Smithsonian's inaugural visitor experience strategy, which addresses all visitor touchpoints across the Smithsonian's 19 museums, galleries, and a national zoo.

The Smithsonian is the world's largest museum and research complex, with 19 museums, nine research centers, and affiliates around the world. Each year we welcome over 30 million visits across our museums. To grasp the totality of these experiences as well as catch important nuances, and begin to build a case for support, I needed to visually depict the experiences of our visitors at our museums. I needed a visitor journey map.

We got started by having a two-day journey-mapping workshop wherein we recorded the end-to-end experiences of Smithsonian visitors. Through the workshop we produced a deceptively simple map that illustrates the before, during, and after visit to the Smithsonian campus and unites us in delivering a "one Smithsonian" experience. As part of this work we established four personas so we could story-tell how the experience of visiting would be different for different types of visitors. These stories make the work we are doing real and personal. The four personas we created are a Spanish-speaking family, a European empty-nester couple, a millennial male visiting from New York City, and 12-year-old Elaine on a school trip.

Out of this workshop we created a first draft of our visitor journey. It was the first time many of my colleagues had ever seen anything like it. It was mind opening. Journey mapping has organically defined and helped people see what my job is, the role and relevance of my office across the Smithsonian, and offers a punch list of specific tasks that need to be addressed in order to improve the visitor experience.

With the journey map I now have a powerful tool that helps visualize the visitor experience. With the visitor perspective in hand my next step was to understand the perspectives of internal stakeholders, including museum executives, department directors, and front-line staff, including volunteers. Over the course of four months I worked to understand what is unique about the visitor experience at each of the 19 museums and the National Zoo. Out of this, we began building a list of what works and what does not at each location and are now putting into place our first batch of improvements.

(continued)

(continued)

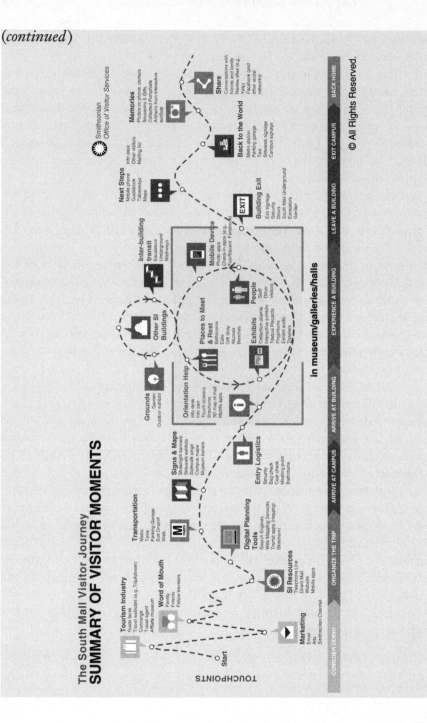

The South Mall Visitor Journey
SUMMARY OF VISITOR MOMENTS

Smithsonian
Office of Visitor Services

Tourism Industry
Guide book
Travel websites (e.g., TripAdvisor)
Concierge
Travel agent
Affiliate museum

Word of Mouth
Family
Friends
Fellow travelers

Transportation
Metro
Taxis
Parking Garage
Bus Dropoff
Walk

Marketing
Email
Ads
Smithsonian Channel

SI Resources
Telephone Line
Direct Mail
Website
Mobile apps

Digital Planning Tools
Search Engines
Web Mapping Services
Transit apps (Hopstop, Busbsus)

Signs & Maps
Streetlight banners
Sidewalk exhibits
Sidewalk signs
Campus maps
Museum banners

Entry Logistics
Security
Bag check
Coat check
Meeting point
Bathrooms

Grounds
Garden
Outdoor exhibits

Orientation Help
Info desk
Info cart
Touch screens
Brochures
3D map of mall
Mobile apps

Inter-building transit
Escalators
Underground
Walkways

Other SI Buildings

Places to Meet & Rest
Bathrooms
Cafe
Gift shop
Alcoves
Benches

Exhibits
Collection objects
Interactive exhibits
Travel Placards
Projections
Exhibit audio
Theaters

People
Staff
Other visitors

Mobile Device
Photo apps
Check-in apps (e.g., FourSquare, Facebook)

in museum/galleries/halls

Next Steps
Mobile phone
Guidebook
Takeaways
Maps

Memories
Photos on phone, camera
Souvenirs & Gifts
Collected Pamphlets
Artifacts from interactive exhibits

Share
Conversations with friends and family
Reviews sites (e.g., Yelp)
Facebook (and other social networks)

Building Exit
Exit signage
Security
Doors
South Mall Underground
Escalators
Garden

Back to the World
Metro station
Parking garage
Taxi
Sidewalk signage
Campus signage

Start

TOUCHPOINTS

CONSIDER GOING | ORGANIZE THE TRIP | ARRIVE AT CAMPUS | ARRIVE AT BUILDING | EXPERIENCE A BUILDING | LEAVE A BUILDING | EXIT CAMPUS | BACK HOME

Leaders who use the journey map to diagnose the experience and its impact on the growth or shrinkage of the customer asset are most successful because they connect the dots between the two in storytelling to the organization. Starting with Competency 1: *"As a result of the experience we delivered to our customers in the last month or quarter or year, here is the growth or loss of our customer asset."* And then continuing to Competency 2: *"Now we will traverse across the journey stages to discover where we helped or hindered customer asset growth."*

This is the beginning a shift from focus only on the survey score, to focusing on the customer life and how it was helped or hindered by the experience delivered. When leaders are consistent and united in how they use the journey framework, it enables them to focus on and prioritize the work of the organization, optimize investments, manage resources most effectively, and improve experiences that impact growth.

And, most important, the customer journey provides the framework to diagnose and care about the "why?" What circumstances causing customers to stay, grow, depart, or diminish their relationship with the company? Using the journey as a vehicle to learn about customers' lives builds an organizational *caring* to want to know the reasons behind their behavior. And this is a game-changer. Why did customers leave? What did we do to cause them to decrease their services? Why haven't they used 50 percent of the software they purchased? By simplifying the outcome of the experience as growth or loss of the customer asset, leaders become more interested in understanding and getting to the bottom of the reasons "why?"

Your Customer Journey Map = Your Business Decision Blueprint

Your customer journey map should be used regularly to provide leaders with consistency in determining organizational needs and priorities necessary for customer-driven growth. Over time, it should be accepted as a united business decision blueprint that can be understood and adapted throughout all levels of the organization. Rigor in addressing employee needs and barriers by examining those issues can then be addressed by customer journey stage rather than silo by silo.

Many organizations say they focus on their customers' experiences but few do the hard work to define the stages of the experiences from the customers' point of view. In the absence of this, all of the operating areas do their own thing, driven by their internal tasks and agenda and scorecard. A lot of work is done, often in the name of the customer, but it doesn't add up from the customers' perspective to deliver a "one-company" experience. The big things don't get systematically improved. We miss the opportunity for the differentiating moments.

However, competency two is not merely about doing touch-point mapping. This is a competency to transform accountability and the language of leaders. And here I insert a little rant and a plea: *please* don't make journey mapping a shiny object that you take on because everyone else is doing it. For this work to be successful, it must connect to leadership language and accountability and communication. Otherwise you're executing an expensive tactic. Those who do so are often left with a lot of post-it notes, binders, and an unclear path on what to do with it all. You don't have to identify yourself.

Done for the right reasons, and in a manageable way, having a customer journey (even a simple one) connects the silos in accountability to customer experiences, and embeds an aptitude for caring why customers stayed or left the business. It provides rigor to understand and step through the lives of customers and pick the places to focus that will have the most impact.

A SIMPLE Journey Map Is Good

When I start this work with clients I always ask, "Have you done any journey mapping?" Often it has been done exhaustively.

This means that every process of every moment of truth has been mapped, which are now documented and in binders on someone's shelf. There are many versions of journey maps created by well-intentioned and enthusiastic teams. But the maps haven't been used to change behavior, focus investments, or drive accountability.

The initial phase of journey mapping we find to be most beneficial is to get alignment on the number of customer journeys that you might want to build *over time*. For example, a company may have customers, employees, contractors, and suppliers. Over time, they may want to build all of them. I suggest you pick *just one* journey to focus on initially to learn a method for journey mapping that works for your company. I've seen too many clients try to map it all at once. What do you do with all of that? It's overwhelming.

Naming the Stages Can Change Your Culture

As you take on journey mapping, make your first action gaining agreement on the names of the stages of the journey. This is **very** important. Naming the customer journey stages begins the shift from independent silo activities to understanding the *complete experiences or objectives that customers are trying to achieve* as a result of their interactions with you. You can kick-start the work by engaging employees and customers in building the stage names and definitions.

It's helpful to think about every stage as a complete experience, with an outcome where the customer ...

- Can state what they were able to accomplish.
- Is clear about the value they received.
- Wants to continue working with you.
- Is compelled to tell others about their experience, product, or service.

ACTION LAB   CUSTOMER-CENTRIC JOURNEY STAGES

What's been interesting as I've been interviewing customer experience executives for this book is that most advocate for a simple journey map, with customer journey stage names that are written from the customers' point-of-view. I couldn't agree more. We universally have the greatest impact when we name stages in this manner. This one activity gives leaders and the organization a way to examine how they currently think about their work and how they communicate and guide business outcomes. At the top of the following figure is the *outside-in* approach to journey stage names. This names stages based on customers' lives. The stage names describe what the customer needs to accomplish, and how he or she would describe what they want to accomplish. At the bottom is the *inside-out* approach. This starts with silo objectives. Which are your customer journey stages most like now?

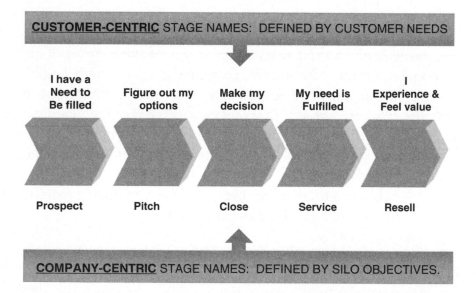

CUSTOMER-CENTRIC STAGE NAMES: DEFINED BY CUSTOMER NEEDS

I have a Need to Be filled	Figure out my options	Make my decision	My need is Fulfilled	I Experience & Feel value
Prospect	Pitch	Close	Service	Resell

COMPANY-CENTRIC STAGE NAMES: DEFINED BY SILO OBJECTIVES.

I suggest that you use the customer journey stages to unite your leaders *before* you jump into touchpoint mapping. Answering the questions below will press your leadership team to agree on how you want to use the journey map to drive change operationally and culturally. We find that leaders who are personally involved in these sometimes mind-twisting exercises are most united in their communication and decision-making. Having these hard conversations before journey mapping can make the difference between a great day had by a bunch of people with Post-it notes and a one-company transformation of communication, decision-making, and accountability.

Accelerating Down the "Customer Experience" Road
Chris Dawson
VP & General Manager, Global Sales and Consumer Experience
BRP – Bombardier Recreational Products

Chris Dawson is Vice President and General Manager, Consumer Experience and Global Sales Division of BRP, Bombadier Recreational Products, where he leads global consumer experience, sales management, go-to market activities, network development, after-sales service, parts, accessories, and clothing for Ski-Doo, Lynx, Can-Am, and Sea-Doo brands, and Evinrude in international markets.

When we highlighted an enhanced customer experience (CX) as a key strategic priority for the company, we clearly touched on a growing "passion point" among our employees: there was already a groundswell of support for the idea of creating the ultimate customer experience. The only issue was that there were too many ideas about how to fulfill this goal, and we knew that we had to be focused.

We spent several months talking with customers in North America and internationally. We involved our senior executive team, including our CEO. Ultimately, we identified five priorities based on consumer moments-of-truth (MOTs): the trial, delivery, service, rider community, and product experience. We agreed to assign certain of the MOTs to our North American team and the others to our international team and established a governance to track our progress ... and we made some

(continued)

(*continued*)

solid progress! For instance, in order to enhance our Service MOT, a cross-functional team was established and reams of data were studied.

The team also took the approach of having each member of the governance team call a number of dissatisfied customers per month, as a means of getting a deeper sense of and better context for what the data was telling us. For the Delivery MOT, our teams conducted interviews with dealers to augment our consumer learning, from which we created an intriguing end state that would transform the delivery experience from "Here are your keys, please sign here" to a "Wow" experience that would build the customers' confidence and anticipation. We then piloted this new process with several dealers and have collected some helpful feedback that will help us refine and focus our efforts even further.

This work of identifying the ideal process flows for customers in these experiences is ongoing, and in parallel we are dissecting the pain points that prevent us from getting to each MOT's end state. It's forcing us to get explicit about uniting operational actions, customer data, dealership and support behavior, and product and services. Down the road, we will have a clear process for each MOT that we can test against cohesively around the world.

We have enormous work ahead. But we now have a path with specifics on how to begin, how to test, and how to assemble teams to get to a desired and articulated end state. Communicating with and engaging our company in this retooling of the customer experience is starting to answer the lingering questions about how we can achieve our CX goals.

Unite Leaders: Why Are We in Business?

You may have already completed the hard work with your leadership team to clarify how your business improves customers' lives. As we get into this work with clients, many believe that they have taken that step. Mission statements abound. But the question I always ask is this: Is that statement used daily as a decision-making lens for uniting the organization in making operational decisions? Do people know it and use it to improve customers' lives and earn the right to growth?

I call this "Clarity of Purpose." Simply put, your clarity of purpose must guide operating decisions. In order to achieve that, it needs to be crafted with the customers' journey at its core.

Without it, people's work will be defined by internal metrics, not by earning the right to customer growth. Without it, the work that comes out of journey mapping is at risk of staying silo-centric rather than guided by a simple understanding of how outcomes should improve customers' lives. Below is a graphic we use to prompt this discussion:

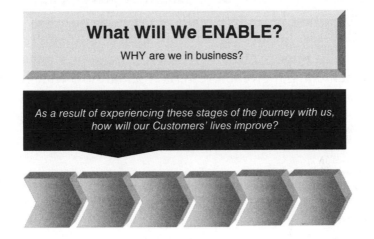

This reminds me of a keynote speech I gave for a large homebuilding company. There were 500 people in the crowd, and while walking around during my keynote (sometimes I think I'm the "Italian Oprah") I started asking people what their job was. "To get the customer to sign the contract," "To get the customer to close faster," "To get the customer to add more options" were the responses I received.

Around the room peoples' jobs were about what was on their scorecard—scorecards that connected to internal goals about the company's growth—not about their roles in improving customers' lives.

We flipped their growth trajectory that day, by reframing their business purpose to "deliver the American dream." This changed everything from how they showed model homes to how they delivered homes to how they kept new homeowners in the loop and excited throughout the building process. Establishing a customer-driven clarity of purpose drove a shift from internal to external goals and netted them a thirty percent revenue growth over the next two years.

How will you improve customers' lives as a result of their journey with you? Focus your messaging on how customers' lives will benefit from working with you versus what you want to achieve in the marketplace, or how large you want to become. This elevates the work of the organization and grounds everyone in taking actions to earn the right to customer-driven growth.

Take this litmus test to determine what you're telling employees is important in their work. Find your company mission statement and give it a read. Is it about how your company will emerge as the leader in your field or become known for a marketplace position to be achieved in x years? Or is it about your higher purpose in improving customers' lives?

Engaging Children in the Library Experience

Alison Circle
Chief Customer Experience Officer
Columbus Metropolitan Library

Alison Circle is Chief Customer Experience Officer at Columbus Metropolitan Library, where she is responsible for the overall library experience and management of 23 libraries and more than 700 staff. Columbus Metropolitan Library is one of the most-used library systems in the United States, and consistently among the top-ranked public libraries.

We know that the younger we engage a child with our library, the more successful they will be in their ability to read at grade level. So we are now mapping a child's journey from their first involvement with us at story time through their progression of our levels of programming. In the library world this is quite innovative.

We are figuring out how to make sure that every touchpoint matters. That includes being able to customize journeys and knowing, within the restraints of privacy requirements, where each child is in their journey with us. This has inspired our exploration of new metrics and how we can gather and learn from them. For example, every child now uses a library card to participate in key programs. In the world of "free" libraries, this is a big step. But it lets us know how recently and frequently they visit or access the library. We also scan as they progress through programming.

And we are developing relationships with schools and their data so we can see how our work impacts these children in their school success.

As a result, we can begin to add value and understand more as a child moves through their journey with the library. We can use this new understanding on continuing to innovate with programming. And we can, over time, establish the correlation between programming, engagement, and childhood progress.

Unite Leaders: Do We Earn the Right to Growth?

This is the fundamental shift that leaders must be united in embracing. And leaders must unite on the priorities along that journey. Otherwise, the work reverts to reactions to silo-based metrics and survey results. The following graphic drives this point home and operationally makes it relevant. By stage of the experience, leaders must be united, committed, and clearly communicate to the organization the experiences customers are trying to achieve. **Experiences that earn business growth are your operational responses to customer requirements** as they do business with you.

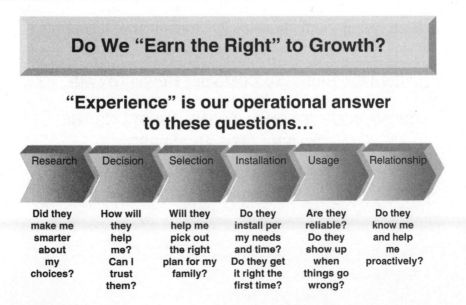

The graphic above lists some of the questions we drafted for a telecommunications client. The questions under each stage are an important part of this exercise because they focus leaders and the organization on what the customer is trying to accomplish within each stage of their journey. This outside-in versus inside-out lens for product development, service creation, and operational execution consistently helps leaders steer the course and guides operational and functional experts to make decisions in their roles.

For example, in product development, do you start with the product or by understanding customers' lives and priorities? Do you build based on what you think or what customers need? Do you build an entire experience for the customer, or is it driven by each silo's report card?

ACTION LAB   **EARN THE RIGHT TO GROWTH**

For each of your customer journey stages draft the questions customers would want answered in each stage as they interact with you. You can then use the journey stages and these desired customer outcomes as a tool for guiding strategic business direction, decision-making, and operational requirements.

"Earn the Right" To Customer-Driven Growth

DEFINE YOUR JOURNEY BY THE QUESTIONS THE
CUSTOMER NEEDS ANSWERED

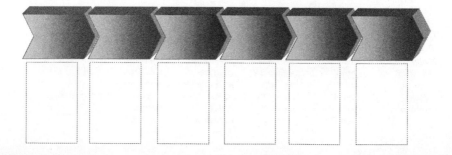

Build a *High-Level* Map to Prioritize the Touchpoints

There are many approaches for touchpoint mapping. My recommendation is always to keep it as simple as possible. I think I mentioned earlier that one client told me they had "Visio blindness" from the hundreds of hours spent mapping every customer process. That's not going to get you traction.

This is what will get you traction: Map the stages and get to the set of initial priority touchpoints along the customer journey. We have great success by first having a session with cross-silo groups of employees to engage them in building a one-company customer experience. As you know, this work sometimes makes people uneasy. They feel we are standing in judgment of their hard work. This type of session brings all the silo-based employees together to establish an understanding that they are all working hard—but they are all working hard separately. It also unites everyone in understanding the stages of the experience, and customer emotions and desired outcomes

In this session we have employees map a first draft of all customer touchpoints and identify what they think are the priorities. We then validate this with customers in a co-creation session where customers come up with new touchpoints as well as identify their priority touchpoints.

Out of these sessions, do not start to map touchpoints. The next step is to communicate a simple roadmap, identifying stages, touchpoints and customer priorities by stage. Later as you establish focus with your leadership team, deeper mapping can occur as you work to solve a particular customer problem or innovate new experiences. But please don't map it all out at this stage—it's boiling the ocean, it's capacity crushing, and without the context of a higher purpose, it will quickly erode perception of value in this work.

Be the Storyteller

Finally, use this information to tell the story of your customers' journey with your organization. Find a creative way to package and introduce the stages as they are established and validated with customers. Use your journey map on an ongoing basis to discuss, stage by stage, the progress made and emerging customer issues and opportunities.

Simple, Visual, Inclusive Communication is Key

Lesley Mottla
Senior Vice President, Customer Experience, LAUNCH
Previously Executive Vice President Global Product & CX, Zipcar

Lesley Mottla is Senior Vice President Customer Experience at LAUNCH. Lesley was part of the management team that developed Zipcar's award-winning customer experience and technologies. She is now Sr. Vice President of Customer Experience at LAUNCH, a start-up devoted to reinventing multichannel consumer experiences.

At Zipcar, we found that simple single-page updates and what I call "scrappy videos" were the most read and watched to keep everyone up to speed and interested. We did a quarterly one-pager talking about progress. These would be a broken-record, tying back to the visual of our customer journey ecosystem and themes for the year so people could see how the work connected. The key was a couple of bullet points explaining the progress with a visual, for example, a picture of our new gas card, which we redesigned to reduce member stress while filling up the tank, highlighting the problems solved for the member and the business.

We also did video vignettes showing the experience before and after it had been improved. These were scrappy, low cost but fun, and often humorous. People would watch them. We held lunch-and-learns where people could come to see how we were redesigning experiences.

We also did "walk in the shoes" activities. For example, all new people joining Zipcar go on a drive, first with an employee and then with a customer. We required people to be part of design efforts, such as our work on the running late-to-turn-in-the car process. Employees would do ride-along rides with customers to observe, participate, or be note-takers. We involved everyone in the company. Engineers were meeting customers, call-center people were doing "ride-alongs" ... everyone was involved in the process.

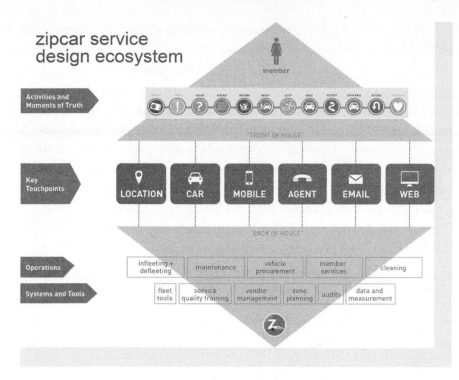

Leadership Shift Required

Competency two's greatest gift is that it resets how leaders hold people accountable. This competency gives leaders a framework for guiding the work of the organization, requiring cross-silo accountability to improve the customer journey and customer asset growth.

It changes leaders' questions from inquiries about silo performance to accountability for customer experience improvement. Over time, when leaders are united in their usage of the customer journey to drive accountability, examine feedback, and establish metrics, the organization will gradually shift to focus on uniting to deliver the experiences that customers prioritize and value most. The company will be motivated to earn the right to growth by improving customers' lives. Your customer journey provides rigor, and a consistent manner to understand and deliver on the priorities your customers value.

However, without alignment among your executive team to regularly review the customer journey and select the few one-company projects that will be supported with collective resources, each group goes off to its own silo and acts separately. Without examining the customer journey to identify critical one-company investments for earning customer-driven growth, annual planning is compromised as each silo picks their project and budgets according to their allotted dollars. But the priority moments for customers are not necessarily identified or improved in a manner that the customer recognizes or feels. The separate incremental projects don't aggregate to improve complete experiences that earn the right to growth.

In short, competency two provides a platform for your customer transformation journey. Once agreed to, you can:

- Line up customer feedback to the stages.
- Connect cross-silo operational metrics by stage.
- Establish reward and recognition that enforces key moments.
- Engage employees to identify what is helping or hindering their efforts by stage.
- Unite leaders in holding teams accountable to experience stages instead of only silo efforts.

Competency Two Impact When Implemented

Leaders in both business-to-business and business-to consumer companies seek clear and simple language they can use to galvanize their organizations in taking actions that lead to customer-driven growth. The customer journey framework provides that talk track. When you do the work with leaders and the company in building the journey and stages, you can eventually have this be the everyday language of your company:

"Now let's traverse across the customer journey so we can understand where we impacted growth or diminished the customer asset. In each stage of the customer journey, where did we earn or lose the right to customer growth? Did we deliver at the priority moments along the journey? WHY is our growth shrinking or growing? What happened in the experience that we delivered to achieve our outcome?"

But like every new language, repetition and practice are necessary to make it a habit. As leaders guide the organization, they can make this stick when they start asking about the customer journey, the customer life. Today because most operations are silo inclined, leaders drive accountability silo by silo. We are glad to comply because silo-based projects are simpler to achieve.

Alignment around experience reorients how work is prioritized, initiated, and completed. It helps to transform how success for your operation is described and measured. Your customer journey map helps to identify priorities and establish focus. It moves customer experience work from "boiling the ocean" (improving all touchpoints) to improving those that matter most in the lives of customers.

Over time, this will evolve leadership language to drive performance along the customer journey, driving accountability to journey stages, not only down the silos. As a result of competency two, leadership questions should change from silo and project movement to customer life improvement. Your customer journey provides a disciplined "one-company" diagnosis into the "why" behind customer asset growth or loss. And it establishes rigor for understanding and caring about priorities in customers' lives.

Focus on the Adoption Experience = Growth

Nick Frunzi
Chief Customer Officer
ESRI

Nick Frunzi is Chief Customer Officer at ESRI, where he directs strategy, metrics, requirements, and resources to enhance customer growth and

(*continued*)

(*continued*)

advocacy and create competitive advantage. ESRI is the world's largest geospatial technology provider, enabling governments, industry leaders, and many others to connect with the analytic knowledge they need to make critical decisions that shape the planet.

In order to understand where customers are in their usage experience with us, we now look inside the behavioral information within our products to know features customers are using and how many are using what was purchased. We are using that to understand a most critical stage for ensuring that value in our products and services is received—our adoption stage.

The adoption stage is the critical stage of the customer experience that occurs after a customer found us, evaluated us, and made a purchase. It is a very short time window where we have to prove value for future growth with them. It is a critical defector pipeline moment.

We now know when a customer enters this adoption stage and we go to work understanding what is helping or hindering adoption. What we learn from these customer behaviors goes to sales, professional services, marketing, training, and product management. Then as a team they work to determine what we should do to help adoption. For example: Is lack of adoption an awareness problem within the company because stakeholders don't know the service is available to them? Is it engagement with the product: that people don't know what to do with the features?

We can now determine for most clients based on their usage, where they are in adoption of our product, and their life cycle as our client. Then we determine the right way to reach out to make them successful. We are working to establish a 30-60-90-day adoption pattern by industry we serve so we can proactively reach out at the right time with the right resources.

Summary

The transformational power in building a customer journey map is to embed a new starting point for the work of the organization. Instead of starting with the silos, the journey guides the organization to align their work to priorities in customers' lives.

The journey gives leaders a communication framework for guiding the priorities of the organization and holding people accountable. When used as a business decision blueprint, the journey map unites leaders in prioritizing, focusing investments and improving experiences to grow the customer asset.

Competency two prioritizes and focuses the organization on the most important touchpoints that impact customers. Used consistently, it helps companies to diagnose and care about circumstances that cause customers to stay, grow, depart, or diminish their relationship.

By using the journey as a vehicle to step through customers' lives, it will start to build in organizational *caring* to know "why?" Why did customers leave? What did we do to cause them to decrease their services? Why haven't they used 50 percent of the software they purchased? By simplifying and stating the outcome of the experience as growth or loss of the customer asset, leaders become more interested in understanding and driving the transformation.

ACTION LAB   LEADERSHIP BEHAVIORS

Every leader I've ever worked with has asked for explicit actions that he or she can take to show their commitment. I've started calling these actions recipe cards because to be successful, they need to be short, simple, and easy to own. To support you with Competency 2: Align around Experience, I have listed some key behaviors for your C-suite to model that will prove commitment with united messaging and actions. Don't take these on all at once. Stair-step them. Get agreement from your leadership team. And then don't stop once you start.

(*continued*)

(*continued*)

Leadership Behaviors to Drive Transformation

Competency 2: Align around Experience

Align the Leadership Team	Give Permission
United Leadership Alignment on the Customer Journey Leaders align on the stages of your customer experience and key 10–15 touchpoints. Change in leadership language and accountability from silo report-out, to driving accountability by experience stage.	**Drive Accountability, and Enable Performance by Experience Stage** Leaders regularly engage with the frontline and behind-the-scenes folks to discuss by stage: what is hindering their work, what is impacting customers? Develop hiring and development tools and support for employees by stage of the experience.

Prove It with Action

United Leadership Decision-Making: Code of Conduct.

Unite leaders to agree by stage of the experience: What will you always do to honor customers or partners? What will you never do to dishonor, disappoint, or distrust them?

Communicate and Reward Decisions.

Free employees to make decisions guided by your "code of conduct" of what you must always and never do by experience stage. Reward for decisions made.

Competency Three: Build a Customer Listening Path

BUILD A CUSTOMER LISTENING PATH.

Seek Input and Customer Understanding, Aligned to the Customer Journey.

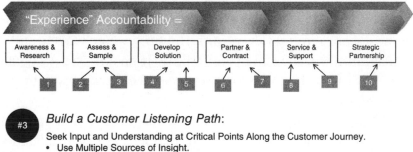

"Experience" Accountability =

| Awareness & Research | Assess & Sample | Develop Solution | Partner & Contract | Service & Support | Strategic Partnership |

1 2 3 4 5 6 7 8 9 10

#3 *Build a Customer Listening Path*:

Seek Input and Understanding at Critical Points Along the Customer Journey.
- Use Multiple Sources of Insight.
- Tell the Story of Customers' Lives.
- Unite Decision-Making and Focus.

Definition: Customer Listening Path

Listening to customers and caring about their experiences is achieved through embedding a competency inside the organization to tell the story of customers' lives. Storytelling across the customer journey is made possible by building a customer listening path.

Your customer listening path will unite leaders and the organization in understanding experiences that impact customer growth or loss. With this competency you build a one-company method to present customer feedback to tell the story of customers' lives. The role of the chief customer officer (CCO) is to engage the organization in united storytelling and focused prioritization of actions.

As you build out your listening path, your customer journey provides the path for storytelling. That is why getting agreement on simple journey stages is so important. Those stages allow you to collapse multiple sources of information, such as feedback volunteered from customers as they interact with you, survey feedback, social feedback, experiential listening and other research to tell the one-company story of customer interactions with you across their journey. You can tell the story of customer perceptions of their experience and value received by stage—as they experience your business. When you present this cohesive view, you can then unite the organization to align decision making on actions that will have the most impact.

This approach helps to reduce the pressure on the survey as the *only* metric that the company focuses on and discusses, reducing the debate about survey results, the survey mechanism, and its connection to revenue and profitability. It enables survey results to be part of a balanced understanding of experiences delivered to your customer.

This one-company approach to diagnosing and focusing on priority actions contrasts what happens today inside most well-intentioned organizations as they review and react to survey results. See if any of this sounds familiar: As results come in separately from surveys, data reports, and social media, they are handed over to an operating area or silo and instructed to "go work on it." Every silo or geography or channel determines how to use the information. Then each interprets the results and plans actions. What happens next is:

- Every leader interprets the results and actions specific to their operating area. Action items are often selected independently, with the focus on survey questions perceived to "belong" to a particular silo.
- The department that has the survey results handed to them in order to "go work on it" completes some action inside their own area, and then reports back at the next meeting.

These well-intentioned efforts make it look like issues are being attended to, but rather than completely improving experiences, many independent projects chip away at one dimension of the experience. A lot of energy is expended with small incremental customer experience improvement.

As you know, broken and unreliable customer experiences are often the result of many things across the operation not working exactly right. For example, billing is a challenging customer experience not just because of what the billing department does. Communications, sales, marketing, operations, IT, and billing all play a role in what the customer ultimately experiences. Customers experience a company across the operation, not down the silos. Doling out issues by silo to interpret survey results and take actions must change to achieve experience accountability and customer-driven growth.

ACTIVE Listening Helps Students with Loan Repayment

Brenda Wensil
Chief Customer Experience Officer
US Department of Education – Federal Student Aid

Brenda Wensil is the Chief Customer Experience Officer at the U.S. Department of Education—Federal Student Aid. Wensil established the

(continued)

(*continued*)

first-ever role in customer experience for the federal government. She is an executive leader in the U.S. Department of Education's Federal Student Aid, the largest single source of funding for postsecondary education in the United States, and a member of the organization's executive operating committee.

Our customers are students and parents borrowing money for education. This equals about 40 million students with loan values of 1 trillion dollars. Over the past couple of years, repaying loans for our customer has been a growing concern. Either the wrong payment plan is set up initially or the student doesn't get the job or salary they had hoped or they weren't prepared to start paying once the six-month grace period of non-payment after graduation ended.

We knew we needed to figure out a way to be proactive in understanding student issues with repayment, not just listen after the fact that students and parents were struggling. So we have added a dimension to how we "listen" in order to reach out to students and parents before repayment becomes an issue. Going into our database of students we have begun using predictive modeling and customer data to help us identify when students are:

- Graduating: This starts the clock on a six-month grace period before payment begins.
- Before the repayment grace period ends.
- The first time they don't make their payment or are late.

Getting buy-in to do this was an effort, because it required an infrastructure to be proactive. We had to really work to get the organization to pay attention to being proactive. I had to, for example, work with my business operations counterpart to allocate resources to work on this. Pushing out an e-mail to a student borrower before they get into trouble on their loan was not something we were used to doing.

To get the go-ahead, we started small. We had to prove that proactive outreach would have a positive result for both the student and on the income side of our work. For the student, the benefit is that they stay ahead of defaulting, which brings with it a host of financial issues that haunt them as they are beginning their independent life. For our administration, creating options for these students where they could repay with comfort drives income rather than defaulting loans.

We did some early analytics by taking a very small slice of this student population and tested the approach of proactively watching student behavior and then reaching out. We started small and watched results to make sure we were on the right path. This effort immediately returned a lift in student participation and a reduction in loan defaults for the test students! More than 50 to 60 percent of students getting these e-mails are opening them, and more than 10 percent of those opening the e-mails are signing up for an alternate payment plan. By proactively listening inside our database, we are able to help students start out on the right foot.

Be the Storyteller: Unite Feedback to Tell the Story of Customers' Lives

The role of the customer leadership executive is to engage leaders and the organization to want to be a part of one-company storytelling and prioritization of actions to earn the right to customer-driven growth. *Storytelling across the customer journey is a transformational element in Competency 3.*

Your guide to build this new state of customer listening and storytelling is prescribed in the three actions below. Through assembling customer listening from multiple sources to build your customer listening path, surveys are combined with other sources to drive convergence on critical issues. Establishing a method for consistently trending real-time issues as customers volunteer feedback adds volume to crystallize more clearly where pain points or opportunities lie.

This approach gives you, the storyteller, much more granular and impactful customer information for storytelling, and removes the burden of trying to convince people to take action from survey data alone. You know the debate about efficacy of the survey collection tool or the sample size or the customers surveyed, and you know the conversation: often as much time is spent in debating the score as in taking ownership of the problems.

Here are the three actions to build your customer listening path:

1. Collect feedback from multiple sources to tell the comprehensive story of customers' lives. When multiple sources of

feedback point to the same issue or opportunity, we see a halt to company debate. There is power in convergence.

2. Build one-company categorization of issues, so that when collected across the company, they roll-up to volumes that command attention.

3. Present information from multiple sources by stage of the experience. This is a game-changer, as issues and opportunities will always be in reference to customers when they are presented in this manner.

Storytelling Resource One: Aided or Quantitative Feedback

Aided feedback means prompted feedback. Customers are asked and their responses are tabulated and quantitatively presented. Surveys of every category fall into the aided feedback category. Pop-up surveys on your website and any other vehicle for asking feedback that originates from your organization is considered *aided*. Today, many companies are executing relational surveys, which ask about the end-to-end relationship with the organization, as well as transactional surveys that inquire about a specific priority experience or touchpoint.

As you well know, there are also many other survey efforts that begin across the organization for the purpose of finding out how a product went over, or a campaign, or another question that needs to be answered, driven by a question within an operating area. These are frequently conducted independently of one another, often tapping customers multiple times, and possibly causing survey fatigue.

When the data comes in, it is investigated, cross-tabulated, and analyzed by survey question and by silo. These well-intentioned actions don't necessarily result in improvements that deepen customer engagement and growth. Rather, they frequently drive mass numbers of incremental improvements from within silo walls, driven by silo scorecards and survey targets.

This may make sense inside the silos that are working to meet their individual metrics. But it does not make sense to customers.

Establishing a Baseline Before Setting Targets

Aisling Hassell
Head of International Customer Experience
Airbnb

Aisling Hassell is Head of International Customer Experience at Airbnb, where she is responsible for the global customer experience. Airbnb is a community marketplace for people to list, discover, and book unique accommodations around the world in more than 34,000 cities and 190 countries.

We have built out both the guest and host journeys and are driving how we build customer listening aligned to the stages of those journeys. At Airbnb we call the stages "frames" as our founder was intrigued by the discipline of Disney and the notion of framing each experience. As we have built out our Net Promoter copyright system, for example, we have prioritized our listening posts according to key frames in the host and guest experience. Our goal is to map key themes from customer feedback and drive continuous improvement frame by frame.

During the early stages of building our listening system, surveys and the analytics behind them were done differently throughout the organization. The great thing is that we have always been keen to hear from our customers. The downside was that, for all the feedback coming in, there was no aggregation point, making it difficult to identify priorities. In addition, we lacked qualitative insight to advance our understanding of the meaning behind the scores. Where there were comments, it was an intensely manual process to decipher key themes, with what we call "air dives" done by individuals within the customer voice team. So overall, we had a lot of feedback but challenges in gaining insights from it.

We now have united our approach company-wide. However, a challenge we continue to grapple with is setting targets for performance. There is nervousness about picking a specific Net Promoter Score (NPS) number, which makes sense as we have yet to establish a benchmark. The goal this year is to establish our NPS baseline performance and make sure that everyone is on the same page before we go crazy with target setting. We need to build out the discipline for that process first.

(continued)

(*continued*)

At the end of the day, we make advances by putting the feedback into categories, aligning it to the journey or frames as we call them, and driving change. The first step is to get everyone comfortable with the new data, processes, and tools. The second step is to get people focused on driving change based on the insights. By focusing in this way, we know we will continue to make Airbnb a compelling experience for our hosts, guests, and employees.

Storytelling Resource Two: Unaided Feedback or Qualitative Feedback

Unaided feedback provides real-time trending on customer issues as they are occurring. Unaided feedback is the constant flow of comments, insights, and issues your customers and partners volunteer to you. Unaided feedback also includes looking inside your data to understand customer behaviors across the stages of their experience, to identify trends, opportunities, and customer at-risk experiences. These are powerful, untapped resources that many organizations haven't yet taken full advantage of. The story from Brenda Wensil above is a great example of the power of using customer behavioral listening to positively improve customers' lives.

Through every interaction point with your customers, they are likely giving you feedback. But because unaided feedback collected independently throughout the organization, often with inconsistent categorization, most companies don't harness the power and volume of this information to pinpoint opportunities. Storytelling is weakened when this information is missing.

What I see when we start this work is that companies who do capture volunteer customer feedback can't prove its impact because it can't roll up to a consistent trend of issues or opportunities. The call center has one categorization they track and report, marketing has their own, and sales has their own. Social media is often reported separately with yet another categorization. Each comes as an independent report, and none of it is pieced together.

I call the opportunities for capturing unaided feedback "listening pipes." You assuredly have many of these pipes with varying volumes of feedback. Remember that volume and convergence are key here, so pick the few highest volume listening pipes that give you those results. And pick the pipes where it will be simplest to put in a common categorization so results can converge from multiple sources. Here are a few sources to consider:

- Customer behavior data in response to experiences, products, services
- Call center volunteer feedback
- Social media on your customer boards and external sites
- Warranty or claim experience volunteer feedback
- Website voluntary feedback
- Return experience voluntary feedback

The power of unaided or volunteer listening is that it will change storytelling from a few customer letters read at meetings to issues trending in volumes that cannot be ignored. What is key here is to pick two to three listening pipes with the most volume so that trends cannot be debated.

The Human Voice of the Client

Scott Dille
Senior Vice President and Director of Client and Employee Experience
Northern Trust

Scott Dille is Senior Vice President and Director of Client and Employee Experience at Northern Trust, where he leads research, design, and measurement of the client and employee experience. Northern Trust is a global leader delivering innovative wealth management, asset management, and asset servicing to corporations, institutions, and affluent individual and families.

We learned early on that earning credibility for this work and gaining consensus and support meant that sometimes we needed people to hear the voice of our client. That means delivering clients' views without

(continued)

(*continued*)

filters or interpretation. We wanted employees to see and hear our clients talking about their lives, their needs, and where we fit into their lives as their wealth manager.

To accomplish this, the team met with a handful of clients individually and created videos as they told their stories. Our people benefit from seeing and hearing clients talking about their personal histories, families, work, passions, and expectations of Northern Trust. These have been especially powerful for many of our employees who don't have direct contact with the clients they serve. For example, back-office employees, who execute transactions such as clearing trades, may spend their workday on a series of specific operational tasks related to managing clients' wealth. Putting a face and a voice to a client creates an emotional connection and a better understanding of the needs and aspirations that employees are helping to fulfill.

I want the human voice of the client to be a means of spurring communication and moving from talk to action. And it is. This approach has also been very successful in engaging our management in staying close to understanding clients' lives and changing needs. Our client videos and transcripts give managers resources for setting business priorities that have the client at their center. To present a balanced view of client experiences, when we have a metrics story to tell, we now include the human voice of the client to create empathy and have people walk in the clients' shoes.

To illustrate the power of this medium, two client videos were shown recently at a meeting of our board of directors and executive leadership team. Their reactions while watching showed us what an impact they had. Now, when we present the human voice of the client, we stand aside and let the client do the talking. As we listen and watch our clients tell us what they need in their own voice, it puts all of us on the same side of the table. Instead of debating priorities or metrics, employees are hearing directly from clients, and that helps to clarify priorities and focus.

Storytelling Resource Three: Experiential Listening

Experiential listening steps your leaders and people in your company through experiences your customers go through.

The goal is to have people see the outcome of the silos, channels, and operational areas working hard, but working separately. Or for them to see the outcome of experiences built from an inside out versus outside in focus. Have employees sign up for accounts, buy a product, change their address, or file a claim. In an organized fashion, establish a required process for people in your company to have to do the things you require customers to do. Establish a "Be a Customer" executive immersion process such as what Adobe adopted, noted in the case study below. Experiential listening is an accelerator to action.

You can also bring customers to life through audio or videos or through engaging personally in listening sessions. The goal is to take the customer off the spreadsheet and build empathy and drive action by thinking about the person at the end of your decision-making.

For many years now, around the world, we've been having executives call customers who left the business or whose engagement with the company has lapsed. The point is to put the voice of the customer in their ear. This always works because it is a personal contact between the leader and the customer. After these calls, we often hear "Why haven't we talked about this before?" regarding an issue or opportunity they heard from a customer. Most likely it *had* been brought up before, but as data, surveys, or metrics. The customer had been cut out of the equation.

You will change your culture with experiential listening. Once you make it part of your storytelling arsenal, you will find that there is no end to the creativity you can employ to take customers off spreadsheets and dashboards and make their experiences real and understood.

When we bring up the idea to leaders that they should call lost or lapsed customers, it is often met with fear and worry: fear that they won't be able to field the call and worry that they'll get irate customers on the other end of the line. Actually the opposite usually occurs. When customers or clients are called and the leader introduces who they are and why they are calling, people are thunderstruck. The conversation goes organically from there.

Below is an Action Lab with some tips on how you can begin your lost customer calling process.

Lost and Lapsed Customer Calling Process—Some Tips and Guidelines

It's important that leaders do not consider this a sales call. While winning back the customer may be an outcome, this call is to listen, learn, and express empathy and caring.

1. Initiate the Conversation.

Acknowledge that we know they have stopped or lapsed interacting with us, and we are so sorry. Can you please tell us what happened?

LISTEN TO UNDERSTAND

3. Earn the Right to Help

Ask if they would accept help to resolve any issues?

Have a variety of personalized options leaders can extend.

PROVE COMMITMENT

2. Probe for more Details.

"Would you be willing to tell me more about your experience?

Repeat back what was heard. Clarify specifics if possible.

DISPLAY CARE & EMPATHY

4. Close the Conversation.

Repeat how sorry you are, and thank the customer.

If follow-through was promised, reiterate next steps.

END WITH HUMILITY

Build Your Customer Listening Path

In competency three the work is to follow the customer journey stages to create a one-company listening path. By leading executives and company members experientially through the customer journey, *improving customers' lives motivates the work*. Storytelling using multiple sources of information and visual and experiential learning drives actions to improve unreliable experiences and uncover innovation opportunity.

This path using multiple sources of customer insight will minimize the debate about the efficacy of the survey collection tool, and curtail challenging debates that put off action and accountability. Surveys are a necessary part of the storytelling in a customer listening path. But don't let surveys alone tell the story of your customer experience and be the driver and motivator of why people act. This is what prompts the debate on the score, the quest for the score, and the diminishing language about customers' lives.

The guidelines below will enable you to start building a one-company customer experience story. We are seeing consistently good results when these are followed because they (a) simplify the data into storytelling, (b) use a consistent framework to align and unite leaders and the organization, and (c) converge multiple data sources to illuminate the few things that matter most to customers versus the many things that matter most to company silos.

1. Build a blend of quantitative and qualitative information to tell the story of customers' lives. Collect feedback from multiple sources. Don't rely on survey data alone. Unite aided feedback, gathered when a customer is invited or prompted to give feedback or respond to a survey, with unaided feedback, which customers volunteer daily.

Assemble survey results in concert with multiple sources of customer insight to provide customer understanding. Survey data should serve to validate numerically what you are already aware of through the real-time feedback received. When aided and unaided feedback point to the same issues/opportunities, we see company debate halt on survey scores. That is because multiple sources point to the same thing. There is power in convergence.

2. Build one-company categorization of issues for unaided feedback, so that they roll-up to volumes that command attention. Many companies capture this powerful information, but it is in separate buckets throughout the operation. The call center has one categorization they use and report, marketing has their version, and sales has their own. Social media is reported separately. Each comes as an independent report, and none of it is pieced together. One-company categorization of issues/reasons and capture is key to rolling up information in volume. Volume in unaided feedback is a strong tool in storytelling because it will show real-time trends.

3. Make it human. Practice experiential listening, the same method that Adobe uses with their Leadership Immersion or that Northern Trust Bank uses with their "human voice of the customer" audio and video. Don't present from a spreadsheet. Take customers off the spreadsheet by stepping people through hearing calls, watching videos, having to log in to a complex site, or seeing the spaghetti bowl of action steps required to sign up for a trial.

4. Present information from multiple sources by stage of the experience, rather than by survey question. This presentation is a game-changer, as explanations of issues and opportunities always begin by being grounded in where they exist in the customers' experience with you.

CUSTOMER LISTENING PATH...

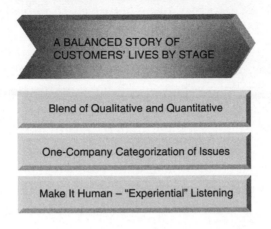

A BALANCED STORY OF CUSTOMERS' LIVES BY STAGE

Blend of Qualitative and Quantitative

One-Company Categorization of Issues

Make It Human – "Experiential" Listening

Leadership Shift Required

Conversations and focus on customers are frequently tied to the cycle of survey results. Presentations of the scores and score analysis drive a flurry of debate and project plans. This is followed by a steep decline in conversations about customers in the periods between survey results. Focus on customers starts up again with the next round of survey results. Sound familiar?

This staccato focus on customers randomizes and exhausts people. It embeds the score-chasing mentality and allows attention to customers' lives to lapse for long stretches of time in between survey result presentations. Most important, leadership messaging on customer-centric efforts is inconsistent, as they often spike around score time but then revert to business as usual.

There must be a shift to break this cycle. Leaders should want to traverse the customer journey on a monthly basis to understand the real-time emerging issues. They should keep their focus on earning customer asset growth by receiving and experiencing a multidimensional story told to them of the customers' lives. Conversations about customers should extend beyond the time when the survey is fielded and the results are reported.

With this, competency leaders and the organization will become personally involved in understanding customers' lives as a constantly refreshing source of information organized by journey stage. They will be able to more simply understand customers' lives not only through data, but also experientially and with a connection to customer behavior and growth. That common path will galvanize leaders to focus on the few key areas of improvement to earn the right to customer-driven growth.

Executive Immersion in Customers' Lives

Lambert Walsh
Vice President & General Manager, Global Services
Adobe

Lambert Walsh is Vice President and General Manager at Adobe, where he leads Adobe's efforts to retain and grow long-term relationships with customers and partners across all segments and lines of business. He has led customer success at Adobe since 2007.

For Adobe's business I've always been a strong advocate regarding Adobe's customers being more than numbers on a page, metrics of revenue bookings, or dollars on a balance sheet. We strive to never lose sight of our customers' humanity and their understanding of what they expect from Adobe.

Our transition to a cloud services provider has heightened the urgency and criticality of customer retention; however, we recognized the importance of immersing leaders and teams across Adobe in our customers' experience long before that change in our business model. We originally focused on gaining a greater understanding of customers with data and information, and found we could have moderate success and make real changes for our customers based on the results of surveys and feedback. That said, Adobe is a company with deeply passionate customers, and we knew we needed to do more. We started the Customer Immersion Program in 2011, with the idea that we had to throw back the covers on all of our work and immerse ourselves in understanding what it was like to be an Adobe customer. We had to engage ourselves personally in our own customer experience.

Every VP was required to go through the Immersion Program, with financial incentives attached to going through the program and becoming personally involved in solving some of the issues encountered. Like any change initiative, the significance of the program wasn't immediately apparent to some, while others jumped in right away. We took a first step with the immersion program because it was our opportunity to humanize the problems customers were having; to take customers off the pages of scorecards and metrics sheets and act with greater urgency to understand the customer experience and respond to their needs. Here's some of what we learned:

- Many of our leaders and managers didn't know firsthand what it was like to be an Adobe customer. They didn't access products or services through the same channels as customers, so they didn't always understand that certain policies or business processes might have unintended implications for customers.
- The data alone isn't enough. Once people walked in the customers' shoes, bigger changes began to happen more quickly.
- Immersion exercises needed to run the gamut from simple to difficult. Participants do all the things customers do every day, like signing up for an account or accessing services. The program works. We started seeing senior leaders who had completed the program then go on to sign up their teams across the company to get more real-life, firsthand customer perspective.

Since its launch, we've extended the Immersion program to leaders across Adobe—more than 2,000 people have completed a version of the program. We knew we were having impact when people started coming to me asking for the next phase.

Our CEO champions the continuation of these immersion experiences so that we continually help leaders understand how they and their teams positively impact the customer experience. Through this process we're able to make explicit links. For example, with Legal the link may be the wording and terms of a contract. With Human Resources, it could be establishing a hiring profile; with Finance it could be more along the lines of making billing systems more simplified and intuitive. The customer experience is a shared responsibility; it's not simply the job of Customer Care.

Competency Three Impact
When Implemented

Today, what we often see is silo-based dissection of customer feedback or independently built feedback mechanisms. These drive fractured solutions and actions and may give a false-positive that customer issues are being resolved. Survey result dashboards built with the good intention to inform and drive action are dissected by survey question rather than by stage of the experience. And each silo dissects the questions with their own bias on actions they can take to increase the lift of the survey score.

A balanced understanding of the customer experience achieved through multiple sources of customer information will engage leaders and the organization to understand customers' lives and focus on actions to earn the right to customer asset growth.

The outcome of this competency will enable you to:

- Tell the story of customers' lives, with the journey as the path for storytelling.
- Present a balanced picture of the current customer experience.
- Enable one-company focus and accountability on priorities.
- Guide complete customer experience solutions informed by multiple sources of customer insights.
- Eliminate reactivity from squeaky-wheel issues.

Through building a constantly refreshing customer listening path, you will reinforce understanding and awareness holistic customer experience to enable focus and prioritization. Combining aided with unaided listening will identify difficult-to-refute opportunities that require executive commitment, resources, and accountability to drive customer asset growth. Through repetition, these conversations will become a natural part of the cadence of everyday conversations.

"Stage by stage of the customer journey, we will now experience what our customer has experienced in real time this past month or quarter or year. In Stage 1, here are the issues emerging from the unaided or voluntary feedback customers gave us as they were interacting with us through our call centers, website, stores, and so on. In Stage 2 ... "

"For Stage 1, here are the survey results that validate the real-time issues we are seeing trend in stage one. In Stage 2 ... here are the survey results that validate the real-time issues we see trending. In stage 3 ... ".

"Now let's look at the experiences in which customers were disappointed that trended in complaints and/or survey results. In stage 1, let's look at the website page that spiked complaint trending this month. In stage 3, here is the page of the contract related to the trending issues of customer confusion."

ACTION LAB   TAKE STOCK OF CURRENT LISTENING

As a first step to modifying or building your listening path, I encourage you to take stock of all efforts going on throughout the organization. Understand your current customer feedback experience. This is how you ask for feedback, receive it, and communicate with customers what you've learned and how you've acted on their behalf. Here are common actions taken by clients as they plan their one-company listening path and evaluate their existing customer feedback experience:

1. **Inventory the volume and schedule of all surveys being sent.** This can be a painful process, but it is also necessary. Find all of the surveys being sent from marketing, the call centers, product development, partners, and so on. In every silo's pursuit of becoming customer centric, the cumulative effect may be causing survey fatigue and frustration to your customers who are receiving them. Take an inventory of all the surveys that go out to customers and when and why. This

(continued)

(*continued*)

action is always one of the first actions we take as we build a listening path for a company.

Many well-intentioned survey efforts are silo-initiated for the purpose of finding out how a product went over, or a campaign or another question that needs to be answered. These are often done separately from one another, and are not usually guided by the customer journey to manage timing or prevent survey fatigue. Put in checks and balances to survey for the right reason, at the right time as one-company.

2. **Organize all surveys by stage of the customer journey in which the customer receives it**. Even a basic set of journey stages is okay here. What you need to see is where there is surveying overlap and, most important, you need to see what your customer sees and experiences.

3. **Examine the methodology for the various surveys. Align to a one-company methodology.** Do you have any surveys that have been building for years, with questions being added here and there from interested parties? I call these the kitchen-sink surveys because they have so many questions that have been bolted on over the years. Are the scales for the surveys consistent? Are some measuring customer satisfaction, some measuring customer effort scores, and some measuring NPS©?

4. **Know the options available to gain customer insight in addition to customer surveys.** For example, is "humanizing" research part of your effort to understand customers' lives? Human-centered design starts with understanding the motivations and emotions that customers are experiencing. This means watching customers in their natural environment using your products or trying to accomplish tasks that your business can assist them with.

This customer observation leads to the identification and understanding of moments where you need to be deliberate and deliver a reliable experience for customers they may not be able to articulate. These also provide powerful cultural artifacts in videotape footage that can be used in your customer room (Competency 5), with work teams, and in your communication to the organization about customers' lives.

5. **Evaluate your ability to practice fearless listening.** I'm sure you have things that you find move people to action faster than others. Besides having leaders call lost customers, we also hold fearless listening with groups of ten to fifteen customers and company leaders participating in the conversation, sitting at the table with customers, talking face-to-face. We traverse the customer journey and ask three things for every stage: how is it going, how does it make them feel, and what would help them to meet their need in each stage? We coach leaders to be a part of the conversation by asking *only* clarifying questions. And we make video recordings of these sessions. Leaders' connection to customers change when they are involved in these fearless conversations. The memory of the customers' voices sticks with them. It gives them a narrative when they speak to their teams and guide the work.

6. **Find your most recent primary research. When was it last completed?** Customer needs are shifting as rapidly as new phones are released. Millennial customers have constantly changing needs and habits. Social media and technology have changed how customers make buying decisions. When was the last time that you conducted primary research to understand shifting customer trends that impact who they are, what they buy, and what motivates them? To earn customer-driven growth investment in staying relevant to customers' lives is crucial.

7. **Grade how reliably you tell customers what you did with the feedback they provided.** Just as it is important to
(continued)

(*continued*)

market hope to coworkers to inform them of actions taken to improve customer experiences and get rid of roadblocks in their jobs, it's of equal importance to tell customers how you've honored and heeded their feedback. Do you do this reliably? Customers need hope that their feedback is not sent in vain. And consider hearing something in return, a gesture of respect. If they take the time to give feedback and never hear back...well, you already know the answer to that.

8. **Make a hard decision. Can you stop asking and act on what you already know?** One of my clients had been sending out a 32-question survey for over five years. The same issues came up repeatedly yet they kept fielding the survey. In our retooling of their listening path, we stopped completely so we could work on what they already knew were priorities. *Not one customer* asked to be surveyed in that one-year period. Instead we started to market back actions taken to improve their experience. *That* customers did notice.

Summary: Take Stock of Current Listening

- Inventory the volume and schedule of all surveys being sent.
- Using your customer journey, map them to journey stages.
- Examine the methodology for the various surveys. Adopt a one-company approach.
- Gain customer insight in addition to customer surveys.
- Evaluate your ability to practice fearless listening.
- Find your most recent primary research. When was it last completed?
- Grade how reliably you tell customers what you did with feedback they provided.
- Make a hard decision. Can you stop asking and act on what you already know?

Business to Business Listening

Robert Wiltz
Chief Customer Officer
Paris Presents

Robert Wiltz is Chief Customer Officer at Paris Presents, Inc., where his role is to transform the go-to market approach for the company, focusing on customer development and brand building. Paris Presents is a global consumer goods company that creates and distributes beauty products through national and global retailers.

At this point we have not employed customer surveys. Instead we have begun in a nonthreatening way, hearing from the customer at all levels in their organization on areas where we can improve. We are a business-to-business company, with retailers as our customers. Because of this we know our top-tier customers very well and, as is frequently the case, these customers contribute the majority of our revenue.

Because we are transitioning from a transactional and price-based selling approach to a strategic and partnership-driven approach to growth, it's too early to do surveys. Instead, we believe we need to start with listening to customers directly to understand the areas they believe we need to improve in order to provide solutions to their challenges, assisting them to provide the ultimate service to their consumers.

A big part of listening is to ensure that all internal functions are part of the process, and that key management from operations, marketing, and finance consistently go with me to visit customers and be part of the solution. There are very few account calls where sales folks are the only ones present. This ensures that management is hearing from customers at the same time, and that we are all aligned toward the total solution. No filter.

Summary

In competency three the work is to follow the customer journey stages to create a unified listening path consolidating multiple sources of customer feedback and insights. Uniting these multiple sources galvanizes leaders to focus and act on the highest priority and highest impact opportunities. And by leading executives and company members experientially through the customer journey, *improving customers' lives motivates the work.*

Today, as research is conducted and surveys are fielded in organizations, internal customers of the information are the recipients of many presentations on results and insights. Each has its own format in presentation. Each has its own timing. This forces the silo customers of multiple presentations to figure out how to unite the multiple data points they receive.

The well-intended actions initiated that result from all this data don't necessarily make improvements encouraging deeper customer engagement and growth. But because of the multiple projects that come out of this feedback from silos independently, a "false positive" is sent to the CEO, leaders, and board that customer issues are being resolved.

To unite the organization in understanding, prioritizing, and focusing investments, astute customer experience leaders are establishing a one-company listening path that unites multiple sources of information. Combining quantitative or "aided" feedback with qualitative or "unaided" feedback, along with "experiential" listening where people in the company have to do what the customer has to do, is transformative. Companies that are uniting multiple sources of information to tell the story of the customers' experience by stage of the journey brings the silos together in understanding complete experiences in need of improvement or ripe for innovation rather than silo-based splinter projects.

When a complete picture of the customer experience is painted, beginning with the growth or loss of the customer asset, qualitative information to visualize the experience, quantitative data to validate and prioritize, and experiential listening to build empathetic understanding, people move past the numbers to real life. Actions are initiated because they will improve priority customer experiences, not because they will boost survey scores. And that shift … in starting with customers' lives … earns the right to customer-driven growth.

ACTION LAB   LEADERSHIP BEHAVIORS

Every leader I've ever worked with has asked for explicit actions that they can take to show their commitment. I've started calling these actions "recipe cards" because, to be successful, they need to be short, simple, and easy to own. To support you with Competency 3: Build a Customer Listening Path, I have listed a summary of key behaviors for your leaders to take, which will prove commitment with united messaging and actions. Don't take these on all at once. Stair-step them and gain agreement from your leadership team, then don't stop once you start.

Leadership Behaviors to Drive Transformation

Competency 3: Build a Customer Listening Path

Align the Leadership Team	Give Permission
Leaders Commit to a United One-Company Listening Path	**Enable Cross-Silo Experience Understanding and Action**
Agreement to build a one-company customer listening path across the customers' experience.	Transition presentation of customer listening content, from survey or silo-based dashboard to insights by stage of the customer journey.
Combine multiple sources to show patterns and move emphasis from the score to understanding and improving the customer journey.	Advocate cross-company collaboration to improve the experience—not try to get "lift" on a score.

(continued)

(continued)

Prove It with Action

Practice Active Listening: Walk in the Customers' Shoes.

You need to know the life to serve the life.
Be a customer: identify the actions you require
customers to take in key touchpoints across the journey.
Stage timing for leaders to take those actions
themselves.

Walk the Talk.

Stop reactive one-off projects and fire drills started
from anecdotal or incomplete information.

Competency Four: Proactive Experience Reliability & Innovation

Competency Four

PROACTIVE EXPERIENCE RELIABILITY & INNOVATION.

Know Before Customers Tell You, Where Experiences Are Unreliable.
Deliver Consistent and Desired Experiences.

"Experience" Accountability =

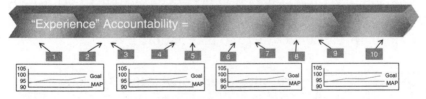

Proactive Experience Reliability & Innovation:

Build the ability to predict performance, rebuild and innovate at key touchpoints.
Make customer experience development as important as product development.

Definition: Proactive Experience Reliability & Innovation

Competency 4 builds out your "Revenue Erosion Early Warning System." It enables your company to know—*before customers tell you*—if your operation is reliable or unreliable in performing at key customer intersection points.

By establishing a competency for managing the process performance of key touchpoints that make or break your relationship with customers, you can start taking actions before customer relationships have eroded, causing customers to depart. These same skills will eventually move the organization beyond managing experience reliability to increasing value through experience innovation.

Leaders need to care about and require reliable operational performance in key customer intersection points. These intersection points along your customer journey impact customers' evaluations of value delivered. They drive decisions to stay, leave, buy more, and recommend you to others. To earn the right to customer asset growth, they require consistency in how they are executed across the channels, the silos, and your business.

Reliability metrics and key performance indicators are the measure of *what you did operationally to earn* the growth or loss of the customer asset. The power here is that these metrics establish the critical connection between reliability performance and customer asset growth. And this connection gets executives' attention. It galvanizes them to take action.

Proactive Operational Metric Tracking

Susan DeLaney
Vice President, Customer Experience
UPS

Susan DeLaney is Vice President, Customer Experience at UPS, where she is responsible for ensuring that UPS customer experience principles are understood, implemented, and upheld at all touchpoints, in all business units and geographies. United Parcel Service serves more than 220 countries and territories worldwide.

We look daily at operational data to identify areas for improvement in our service. Our goal is to identify things that are not meeting expectations and fix them before customers tell us about them. Research has identified operational service elements that are valued by our customers. We need to vigilantly make improvement in these areas to deliver on the service expectations of our customers.

For example, customers ship packages with bad addresses. They may not include an apartment number or the zip code is wrong. Bad addresses make delivery slower. We know that delivering on our time in transit commitment is a critical value driver for customers, regardless of whose fault it is that the package was delayed.

To solve this, we created a project to identify addresses that are incorrect as soon as we have the electronic package information. The goal is to determine the correct address as soon as possible so that once they hit the destination center, they can be scanned and corrected, preventing delivery delays.

By being proactive in understanding, tracking, and managing our performance in critical process metrics, we are making greater traction in solving issues, helping to reduce the effort for customers to conduct business with us and deliver on their service expectations. This demonstrates to our customers that they are valued, reduces their frustration, increases loyalty, and ultimately reduces costs.

Competency four gives leaders actual operational performance metrics that proactively measure reliability of the processes that impact priority touchpoints, before the survey results come in. Using your journey framework and mapping of unaided and aided feedback across the journey, these multiple sources combine to enable informed and balanced decision-making.

For example, in the automotive business, the test-drive experience is pivotal to the car-buying decision. But what most automakers measure is the end result—the number of units sold. They do not put rigor into building a reliable process for test-drives no matter where or when they are requested. Many are not measuring actual operational performance at the dealership in delivering test-drive experience reliability, or at the corporate level in supporting it.

Yet the ability or inability for a customer to test-drive correlates directly to sales. The only available measure is asking the customer much later in a survey, "How did the test drive go?" Many manufacturers don't track or proactively manage operational reliability of the following processes that impact the customer test-drive experience.

- Time to respond to customer requests for a test drive.
- Conveniently located dealers and desired test-drive vehicle availability.
- Time between customer request for a test drive and the drive itself.

Another example is a software-as-service company marketing a very popular game. The focus was on units sold and renewals. Those were the line-of-site metrics executives cared about. But the operational performance of gamers' ability to access and use the game and the stability of the experience were not metrics looked at with rigor. The metrics existed somewhere but they were buried in each silo. Requests for information about users' experiences did not match the urgent requests for information about sales. User experience metrics are now viewed daily, because performance reliability directly impacts gamers' desire to keep on playing, to buy more, and to tell others.

Make Customer Experience Development as Important as Product Development

For customer experience to be considered a core competency of the business as important as product development, finance, marketing, or sales, it needs to be built and honed as a skill. This means having:

- Rigor and discipline for how cross-functional teams explore and understand emerging issues and opportunities.

- A clean and clear process for evaluating and understanding what customers need and value in improved or redesigned experiences.
- A method for building shared processes and metrics to deliver one-company priority experiences.
- Rigor in identifying the key priority experience metrics that are elevated to leaders for regular review.

Most organizations have a rigorous process and discipline for how they develop a product. But there is not the same discipline established for developing and bringing customer experiences to life. The ability to improve or innovate experiences starting with customer requirements is not an inherent skill in most organizations.

The role of the CCO is to work with leaders to determine how to bring the competency of customer experience development and innovation into the organization. What we find works well with many clients is to establish a small center of excellence for facilitating these work groups. An expert (either employee or contractor) in experience design and human-centered design works as the facilitator to make every team effort successful and consistent. Each team follows the same process, beginning with united leadership review of the customer experience where a project and applicable team members are identified. The customer experience facilitators take each team through a one- to six-month cycle of investigating, developing, proposing, and implementing. With this cycle team members learn the skills they can eventually bring to their functional areas.

The five-competency customer-driven growth engine provides you with an evergreen cycle to know, care about, and diagnose what is causing the growth or loss of the customer asset. Once customer experience priorities are identified, this work is to embed the process for evaluating and implementing customer-driven solutions and new standards for operational performance that leaders care about and hold people accountability for.

Making Experience Improvement Reliable

Claire Burns
Chief Customer Officer
MetLife

Claire Burns is Chief Customer Officer at MetLife. She drives the customer-centric strategy and actions to build customer empathy and improve the experience of purchasing, maintaining, and enhancing customer coverage with MetLife. MetLife, Inc., is a global provider of insurance, annuities, and employee benefit programs.

We have a small customer experience practice group in my team. They are supplied as resources to assist operations teams in solving customer experience issues. The skills that they possess are an in-depth understanding of customer experience, user experience design skills, a breadth of skills to be able to influence, encourage collaboration, and drive to an outcome with teams as a resource versus authority.

This team provides rigor and a regular cycle for how we support operating areas in working together to tackle issues. They facilitate mapping of the current state and future state and competitor state. They do a very simple, clunky map of the current experience (no Visio blindness level work!). They bring in customer understanding and research and identify gaps between current and future state, ultimately enabling these operational work teams to prepare their blueprint of the ideal future state. Then they get operational, mapping against current capabilities, identifying investment scenarios. Once the work moves forward, our team continues with them in implementation, ensuring core metrics of the experience are embedded from an outside-in perspective.

These efforts typically start as pilots, in a four- to six-month cycle. This has proven to be a solid way to begin to embed that this work is a competency and to create a regular rigorous process for achieving customer-driven experiences that contribute to growth. It is a journey that requires us to consistently show value and add value.

New work groups will constantly be assembled as issues are put to rest and new ones emerge. Over time, as the most unreliable issues are tackled, the work will mature to focus on experience innovation, beyond experience reliability improvements. What's important to consider in this competency is that it is an ongoing resource requirement that needs consideration. Customer experience and human-centered design facilitator skills will be necessary on an ongoing basis to earn the right to customer-driven growth.

Experience Reliability Reality Check

When we begin this work, most organizations haven't evaluated the reliability of the experience delivered across the entire customer journey. Most are inadvertently delivering a random experience to customers for a number of reasons, which we have discussed before.

- Silos have distinct priorities and metrics.
- Leaders don't unite to build end-to-end priority experiences.
- Issue resolution occurs mostly by silo, driven by survey score reactions.

This is exacerbated by multiple channels and customers' increasing expectations that all of these intersection points sync up with common reliability. That the right hand and the left hand of the organization connect.

ACTION LAB	RELIABILITY REALITY-CHECK

At the beginning of this work, I do an experience reliability check with clients. And that is to ask them to rate the reliability of the one-company experience for each stage of their customer experience. The question is this: "In this stage of your customers' journey, is the experience you deliver consistent and reliable?" Often, the answer everyone agrees on is, "It depends." It depends on the person, the channel, the product offering. This lack of one-company experience reliability impacts growth and profitability. And that is why we need to get leaders to care about the things that cause the "it depends" experience.

We start this activity by having participants walk in the customers' shoes. This is usually a combination of reading quotes, watching videos, or having them "be a customer" prior

(continued)

(*continued*)

to the session, signing up for services or trying to get a trial, and so forth. The reason for this is that most people's definition of good service or good experience is tied to how hard they are working inside their silo. And that's true. People are working hard…separately. And that separate work gets in the way of experience reliability. We use this activity to help people move away from their silo work—to see the total experience as customers do.

How Reliable is the Current Experience Delivered to Customers?

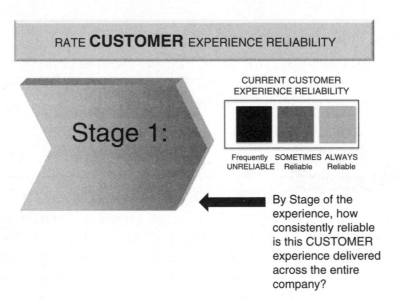

Next, we go stage by stage across the customer journey and ask the group how absolutely reliable that stage is *at all times* in delivering a one-company experience to the customer. The figure above illustrates this process. For example, "frequently unreliable" means it's a real problem area for you. "Sometimes reliable" means that it depends on where the customer interacts. "Always reliable" means this experience is totally managed across the channels, countries, and silos. Then, we mark where the group says the reliability is by stage. Often they rate themselves between the categories of reliability on the continuum.

Most companies are very surprised when they evaluate themselves as "frequently unreliable" on many journey stages. That's because the company and leaders have not had the opportunity to think about reliability the way the customer has. And that is the power of this exercise. It unites leaders and the organization that there is work to be done. And it clearly shows that for complete experiences to be delivered, the silos can't work alone.

After you've completed rating reliability of your customer experience, then go on and rate how reliably you support employees in delivering value across the customer journey. We find that the employee journey rating is just as important as the customer rating, because in that discussion you'll hear root cause issues preventing the front and the middle from being able to deliver value.

How Reliable Is the Support Provided Employees to Deliver Value?

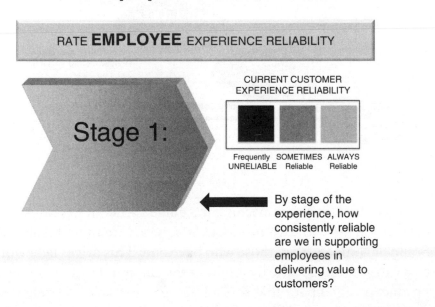

(*continued*)

(*continued*)

Reliability Leads to Customer Desire for Your Experience, and Customer Growth

The following chart is what I call the "stairway to desire." I place it here to make a point about the power of reliability and the current state of most of my clients' customer experiences as we get into this work. (You are not alone!)

I'm introducing a new word for you to consider with this competency, and that is to replace the word "loyalty" with the word "desire." That is because what I've experienced and observed is that "loyalty" can be considered something to go *get* from customers, rather than something to be earned.

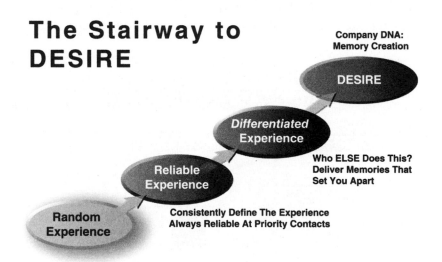

Loyalty efforts can become misguided when it's established that customers with two products or services are more loyal to a brand or company than those who have one. This drives behavior to try to *get* more loyalty by pitching the client to buy that second product or sign up for that second service. Instead of earning the right to growth by delivering reliable and valuable experience, customer loyalty efforts focus on math and actions to get customers to buy more. The focus goes to campaigns focused on upselling and cross-selling to customers.

But you can't earn loyalty without doing the hard work to deliver a reliable experience. That is why I use the phrase "earn the right to grow." If you deliver a reliable experience, your customers and clients will desire to have it again. Desire is an emotion that will earn growth and prosperity for your business. Competency four builds the discipline for doing the hard work to deliver reliability and earn customer desire.

Our First Batch of Improvements

Samir Bitar
Director, the Office of Visitor Services
Smithsonian Institution

Samir Bitar is Director of the Office of Visitor Services at the Smithsonian Institution. Samir is responsible for developing and overseeing the implementation of the Smithsonian's inaugural visitor experience strategy, which addresses all visitor touchpoints across the Smithsonian's 19 museums, galleries, and a national zoo.

Our first batch of visitor experience improvements focused on the visitor pain points we discovered during our journey-mapping workshop.

One pain point was to improve orientation for first-time visitors. Within the Rotunda (principal entrance) of the National Museum of Natural History, the largest natural history museum in the world, it appeared to visitors that two information desks were available to them. In actuality, only one was an information desk prepared to support visitors; the other sold only IMAX tickets. Each year about 3.2 million visitors (40 percent of visitors) stopped at one of those desks. As a result, many unknowingly asked the information person to sell them IMAX tickets. When that occurred, they were sent across the Rotunda through visitor traffic to the IMAX ticket desk 50 feet away. This was neither visitor-friendly nor good for business. In response, one of our first improvements was to redesign floor plans and way-finding—how visitors find their way throughout the museum, including redesigning the Rotunda with *one* centrally located

(continued)

(continued)

information desk where visitors will find all the information and staff necessary to plan a visit, including IMAX tickets.

We also learned that about half of the Smithsonian's 33 million annual visitors sought some level of support in deciding what to do from among the more than 300 daily exhibitions and events; however, not all of them stopped at an information desk. In response we developed a host of products and services including a new Visitor Concierge, a roving cohort of staff on site across the campus who help visitors where they are, rather than sending them to an information desk. And for the 60 percent of visitors who would rather not interact with a staff person, we have developed a new digital product that enables visitors to create personalized visit itineraries. By answering six easy questions we filter, sort, and provide routing to only those exhibitions and events that fit the details of someone's visit. Simple, right? But up until 2014 we were still viewing the visitor experience through a 20th-century lens, and therefore continued to do things a certain way.

And finally, we designed a visitor center. There hadn't been a functional visitor center at the Smithsonian for the past 15 years. Since no one in my role, overseeing the visitor experience from a central office, had been advocating from the visitors' point of view, there wasn't broad awareness among the leadership of the pain points across the on-site visitor experiences that a visitor center could mitigate. Specifically, that it would improve the planning and orientation services desired by Smithsonian visitors to get the most out of their visit to our extensive campus. Articulating what was lacking was a key element in securing support from Smithsonian senior leadership. And our journey map was very instrumental in building a case to gain funding, which we did. So we have now pulled together a cross-discipline team of stakeholders from across the Institution, including users of the space, and have designed and are preparing to open our new Visitor Center.

Social Media and Experience Reliability = Customer Growth

When you deliver a reliable experience, you earn the right to your customers' story through word of mouth. And your customers will come back because they want to have your experience again. Three conditions earn the right to customers discussing their experiences on social media. These lead to new customer growth, free of acquisition cost, and grow volumes of vocal customer advocates marketing the company for you. These are:

1. Was the experience *consistent and reliable*, no matter where or who the customer talked to in any channel?
2. Does their relationship with you *improve their life or business*? Did your actions prove your commitment to them?
3. *How does it feel* for the customer to do business with you? Honored, distrusted, ignored? All of these come out in tweets, reviews, and message boards.

What we know is that the power of social media—either in person or online—has an increasingly high impact on purchase decisions. In both business-to-business and business-to-consumer organizations, customers listening to the reviews and feedback of others who have experienced your business drive their buying decisions. Ninety-two percent of consumers worldwide trust recommendations from friends and family more than any other form of advertising.

92%

of consumers worldwide trust recommendations from friends and family more than any form of advertising. (Up from 74% in 2007)

Source: Keller Fay Talk-Track Report and Word-of-Mouth Marketing Association.

When your experience is unreliable, the most powerful way to grow—positive word of mouth—will suffer. If the experience you deliver to customers is not consistent and reliable no matter what channel or silo or location they interact with, then customers won't vouch for you. That will impact recommendations and organic growth.

Because if your customer can't tell another customer what they get from you, how they get it, how it improves their life, and consistently how you make them feel as a result, then you don't earn their recommendation. You don't own the moment, and at any time they may go shopping for a company that's more reliable. More important, the lack of reliability will send them away.

With social media entrenched now as a shiny object, along with a lot of customer experience tactics, the tendency is for leaders to want to go out and implement the wow moments. But reliability has to come first—otherwise money spent on the wow is a wasted investment. Think of reliability as the foundation. Just moving to reliability in many of your complex businesses such as health care, financial services, or insurance, for example, will make you stand out. In complex industries, **you will differentiate when you are consistent and reliable.**

When I give keynotes I offer an anecdote about a hotel experience: If, when you check into a hotel, they ask you what type of pillow you'd like and the kind of chocolate you'd like at turndown, but when you walk in the room there's hair in the sink and dirt under the bed, all that "wow" is lost in the lack of reliability.

The London School of Economics has determined that there is a 300 percent revenue gain to be had by focusing on reliability versus the wow moments. That does not mean that your version of reliability is mundane. Apple is reliable; they have their own way of doing reliability and that differentiates them. Amazon is a reliability engine. Amazon sold its first book in 1995. If they did not sell, ship, and deliver that book in a reliable way, they would not have earned the right to the over 200 categories that they sell now.

300%

Revenue gained by reducing negative word-of-mouth versus improving positive 'buzz'

Source: London School of Economics Advocacy Drives Growth Study.

The role of the chief customer officer is to drive executive and organizational appetite for wanting to know about interruptions in customers' lives and opportunities for differentiation. The outcome is to unite the silos, simplifying how key customer intersection points are delivered, and facilitating a one-company response to performance issue improvement and experience innovation.

And that means simplicity in how you deliver the information, show its impact, and galvanize leaders into action. For example, with many clients (especially product and sales driven companies) we introduce the priority touchpoints as a "Defector Pipeline."

ACTION LAB	BUILDING A DEFECTOR PIPELINE

For some leaders the idea of a *"Defector Pipeline"* is more easily embraced and advocated for than *"moments of truth."* The defector pipeline identifies the make-or-break moments when proactive management and intervention are required to earn customer

(continued)

(*continued*)

growth. Calling it a defector pipeline invokes an explicit connection to specific customer intersection points that should be invested in. It doesn't sound "soft" and it is a very effective way to engage leaders, especially in very sales- and product-driven businesses.

Building a Defector Pipeline (SaaS example)

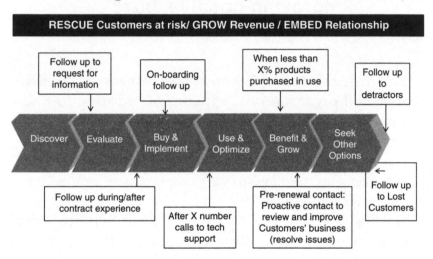

If the term *moments of truth* is not hitting home, try *defector pipeline*. It may do the trick in connecting the dots between customer experience management and growth. For example, if you are missing customer cycle times, which deliver on a key part of your promise, your executives need to know and care that this is happening. **Missing your performance standards in those moments is an early warning system on loss of revenue and growth.**

Leadership Shift Required

When I begin working through the development of competency four with my clients, I ask client companies "Do you focus on process?" The answer is often a groan. Process improvement—the discipline required to build and improve customer experiences—feels like work layered on top of the real work of the business. With this competency, you can shift leadership attitude from work layered onto the business of achieving sales to work that enables the achievement of (more profitable) customer acquisition and customer asset growth.

When you are successful in building out this competency, you will gain the executive mindshare to focus on disappointment or interruptions in customer experiences that lead to departure or diminishment of the customer asset. You will build leadership demand for management of these moments with as much rigor and passion as they track sales goals and revenue. Leaders will require experience reliability because they understand the impact of lack of reliability: value erosion, customer departure, and negative word of mouth.

If you find you need to sell this work, sell it as your "Revenue Erosion Early Warning System." These failures will stack up to drive customers and their contracts, goodwill, sales, and recommendations out the door. This early warning system gives leaders indicators to know when customer asset growth is at risk. Competency four gets you ahead of customer suffering and survey results so you can proactively solve the issues eroding growth and advance priority touchpoints with experience innovation.

Center of Excellence for Customer Growth

Taylor Rhodes
President and CEO. Previously Chief Customer Officer Rackspace.

Taylor Rhodes is President & CEO of Rackspace. He was previously Senior Vice President & Chief Customer Officer. Rackspace is the number-one managed cloud company, delivering open technologies and powering hundreds of thousands of customers worldwide.

(continued)

(*continued*)

We began what we call a Churn War Room in 2008. This was our reaction to the global financial crisis to help small and medium businesses keep their service with us. At the time a lot of small and medium businesses were going out of business or were very challenged financially. We established this war room to determine economically feasible ways to help our financially challenged customers stay with us. Because we had good financials on the value of a customer, we were able to establish thresholds of what we could do to keep a customer and return an ROI, based on calculated lifetime value. Those economics were critical so that we could know what we could do to help a customer remain with us.

We offered this to account managers as a center of excellence where they can get help with these relationships at risk. We staffed this effort with a couple of permanent facilitators, and then added in team members from company disciplines as applicable to the challenge. Our message that resonated was this: work with us to make deliberate and financially viable decisions about who we are willing to let go and when. After the worst was past in 2009, we mothballed this effort, but resurrected it in 2012.

In 2012 we resurrected this effort as teams were encountering install base risks that were not economic, but related to perceived value and service received. We are taking our most knowledgeable and experienced people and supporting the client facing teams to understand and address these issues. This is now more of a process that's understood and regularly called upon as teams are encountering challenges. It is a disciplined process that begins with understanding what customer's love and hate, and the assembly of a team that includes support from finance, pricing, product development, and others necessary. We service over 250,000 customers and we learn a lot in that process. We have aggregated that learning to help teams and bring wisdom to saving customers. Because it has had an impact in reversing trends, this is now a permanent function. We are providing our account managers with a center of excellence where they can get help and make deliberate financial decisions to impact earning the right to Install Base growth.

Competency 4 Impact When Implemented

As a result of this work, you will have established and embedded a reliable process for tracking operational performance to know, before customers tell you, your performance in delivering reliability and value.

Once customer experience priorities are identified, this competency will give you the process for evaluating and implementing customer-driven solutions and new standards for operational performance that leaders care about and hold people accountable for. *Competency 4 puts you ahead of survey results, which is where you need to be to proactively drive customer asset growth.* As a result leaders can clearly see operational performance patterns to diagnose the reasons for customer asset growth or loss. The power of these multiple sources coming together is that they start with the customers' lives, not the spreadsheet, and not the survey score.

> *"For Stage 1, it's no wonder complaints are spiking. The three operational metrics most critical to the customer experience are not meeting their minimum acceptable performance standard. Here is where we are interrupting customers' ability to get value from our experience. We see here in Stage 3 that we are tipping below our standard performance for the cycle of getting a proposal to the customer. Before this turns into an issue for our clients, let's get a team on this situation."*

As a result of this competency, customer experience improvement (CXD) will become a competency as understood and required as new product development (NPD). Skilled customer experience development and innovation approaches will guide cross-functional teams toward successful and rewarding outcomes for improving customers' lives. Prioritized opportunities will follow a consistent path, beginning with united leadership review of the customer experience where a project and applicable team members are identified. Each team will follow a one-to six-month cycle of investigating, developing, proposing, and implementing. With this cycle, team members learn the skills they can eventually bring to their functional areas to continue embedding this discipline across your organization.

Summary

Competency four builds out your "Revenue Erosion Early Warning System." It enables your leaders to know—*before customers tell you*—if your operation is reliable or unreliable in performing at key customer intersection points.

With this competency you will elevate the importance of cross-company reliability as a condition for customer asset growth. Guided by your journey framework, these are the opportunities for reliability and future differentiation in four categories of customer touchpoints:

1. Managing customers at risk
2. Responding to customer needs
3. Strengthening bonds with relevant value added
4. Earning the right to revenue growth

These are the moments that will most impact your growth. Failure to perform in these moments will disappoint customers when they expect reliability, miss an opportunity to rescue a customer at risk, or lose the chance to add value or expand your share of wallet with a customer.

To earn the right to customer-driven growth, leaders need to embrace and build a discipline to proactively know one-company performance in these touchpoints, and have an agile process for improvement embedded as a competency across the organization.

ACTION LAB   **LEADERSHIP BEHAVIORS**

Every leader I've ever worked with has asked for explicit actions that they can take to show their commitment. I've started calling these actions recipe cards because to be successful, they need to be short, simple, and easy to own. To support you with

Competency 4: Proactive Experience Reliability and Innovation, I have listed a summary of key behaviors for your leadership team that will prove commitment with united messaging and actions. Don't take these on all at once. Stair-step them and gain agreement from your leadership team, then don't stop once you start.

Leadership Behaviors to Drive Transformation

Competency 4: Proactive Experience Reliability

Align the Leadership Team

Require Operational Performance That Earns Customer Growth

Leaders require accountability in key customer experiences to equal their rigor in demanding sales performance. Make Customer Experience Development (CXD) as important as New Product Development.

Give Permission

Commit Resources To Customer Experience Development

Build the competency of a cross-silo customer experience development process (CXD).

Provide resources for cross-functional teams to work the customer experience development process together to improve experiences and operational metrics that drive value and growth.

Prove It with Action

Give Customer Experience Development Time...

Allow the Customer Experience Development process the time and resources for it to become a competency of the organization. Don't abandon it because it takes time.

Reward Cross-Silo Collaboration.

Reward cross-functional teams for complaint reduction and sustainable experience improvement.

7

Competency Five: One-Company Leadership, Accountability, and Culture

Competency Five

LEADERSHIP, ACCOUNTABILITY, and CULTURE

Leadership Behaviors Required for Embedding the Five Competencies. Enabling Employees to Deliver Value.

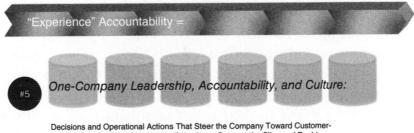

"Experience" Accountability =

#5   *One-Company Leadership, Accountability, and Culture:*

Decisions and Operational Actions That Steer the Company Toward Customer-Driven Growth. United Leadership Behavior to Connect the Silos and Enable People to Act.

Definition: One-Company Leadership, Accountability, and Culture

This is your "prove it to me" competency. For this work to be transformative and stick, it must be more than a customer manifesto. Commitment to customer-driven growth is proven with action and choices. To emulate culture, people need examples. They need proof.

Competency five is the glue that holds the customer-driven growth engine together. It puts into practice leadership behaviors required by a united leadership team to enable customer asset growth.

As you have seen in Competencies 1 through 4—Customers as Assets, Align around Experience, Customer Listening Path, and Proactive Experience Reliability and Innovation—there are both operational actions and behavioral leadership shifts required for success.

Here, we focus on the behavioral leadership shifts necessary in communication, decision-making, and behaviors necessary (over time) to embed them as part of your business engine. These are actions and change management behavior to stair-step leaders from silo-driven agendas to one-company customer journey and customer asset growth priorities. Only then will these competencies become adopted as part of your business engine. Only then will they move from a program to your operational and cultural DNA. Only then will leaders unite in guiding the organization to "earn the right" to customer-driven growth.

Customer culture is talked about by many leaders but misunderstood by most organizations. A manifesto or commitment is stated, but often people don't know how to translate those words to their own performance and priorities. "Commitment" to customers is spoken of vaguely, rather than attached to deliberate operational behavior, such as *"We will go to market only after these 12 customer requirements are met"* or

"Every launch must meet these five conditions, which the field requires for success. We won't launch without them, no exceptions."

You must move beyond the customer manifesto and translate the commitment to actions people will feel proud to follow and emulate.

You must move beyond the customer manifesto and translate the commitment to actions people will feel proud to follow and emulate.

Culture is the action, not the words. It is the consistent behaviors that give people direction on what to model, decisions that are made, and actions that are taken that show that customer commitment is real and not lip service. Competency five gives leaders a rigorous process with which to examine, commit to, and improve customers' lives:

> *"In stage 3, we have three legacy rules that are causing the majority of the complaints and causing more than 50 percent of transactions to require a manager's involvement. We need to remove these 'stupid rules' and let our employees and customers know.*

> *As a result of understanding the current customer journey as a leadership team prior to annual planning, we now have the top five company-wide priorities for next year to focus on to improve our ability to earn customer-driven growth."*

The role of the customer leadership executive is to work with leaders to provide proof that they are committed to improving customers' lives. Moving well past words, a deliberate and united set of actions and behaviors practiced in unison is required.

Our Customer Experience Steering Committee

Kevin Thompson
Vice President Customer Experience and Development
Barney's New York

Kevin Thompson is Vice President, Customer Experience and Develop-
ment, at Barneys New York. His role is to actively manage the highest level
of service standards across all company touch points at Barneys New York,
a leading U.S. luxury retailer, to create a seamless omni-channel brand
experience.

We have established a Customer Experience Steering Committee
with our senior level team. Every month, we sit in a room together, about
25 of us, and we talk about the experience, what we should be doing,
and where we should be learning. We look at other industries besides our
own in these conversations so that we are not limiting ourselves to retail,
and so that we are looking at all the other experiences our customers
are having.

The format varies every month to keep it fresh and to keep the
leaders engaged in an experiential manner, versus a reporting session.
We start with the actions we have recently completed. Then we talk
about focus projects in progress. Since we have five committees working
on focus areas, each led by a senior team member, we also use these
meetings to have these teams present their progress. These teams
are composed of store managers, salespeople, and many throughout
the company, so this is a powerful forum for them as well as for our
leadership team to see the progress we are making and to make united
decisions in terms of guiding efforts.

In these meetings we look at emerging customer feedback and
determine new areas of focus we will add. The steering committee is
the chance for me to identify focus areas—sometimes our CEO agrees,
sometimes there's a lot of debate and we get into things and figure out
the best practice. I would rather have the debate. We put ideas out there
and test them and take the temperature of the Steering Committee.
We then decide as a team and move on it. We have so many things
on the go because we literally had to fix everything—systems, policies,
procedures—we don't have time to waste.

In addition to steering actions and decisions, we always have a portion of this time that engages us in a human way with customers and their
lives. We watch videos of customers. We do group activities to experience

what customers experience, such as our online experience. Sometimes we will assign independent experiences before the meeting, which we then discuss. We sometimes watch Ted Talks about employee happiness and wellness. It's a slightly different format every time. We don't want these meetings to get routine and boring. The goal is to engage our leaders in making united decisions, drive accountability, and improve our understanding of our customers' lives.

Leadership Shift Required

As identified in Chapter 2, "Ensure Role Adoption and Acceleration," three common categories of behavior are necessary as the leadership team works together to build out the five competencies. These categories comprise the prove-it-to-me behaviors that enable a successful transformation. They are the change management building blocks necessary to move past project plan movement to customer life improvement.

MOVE FROM TALK TO ACTION

UNITE THE LEADERSHIP TEAM

How We Will Grow. How We Will Not Grow
Capacity – Culture – Competency

GIVE PERMISSION, BEHAVIORS TO MODEL

Decisions that Prove Commitment
Enable People to Deliver Value

PROVE IT WITH ACTIONS

One-Company Accountability
Congruence in Hiring, Motivation, Recognition

1. **Unite the leadership team.** United leadership team prioritization, messaging, and partnership are imperative for employees to observe and experience, so that they can model this behavior among their own peers. The leadership team must support and enable customer asset growth with consistency.

2. **Give permission and behaviors to model.** Organizational dynamics and communication that are extremely necessary, but often lacking must be addressed, guided by the customer journey framework. This is where you address the human issues critical to building your customer growth engine. How are leaders enabling the organization to work? How are decisions made? Why are people rewarded and recognized?

3. **Prove it with actions.** The leadership team must be united on how they determine investments and prioritize actions. As these decisions are made, the organization must be actively provided with these examples, so they can model the same actions in their operation and roles.

Transformation = Embedding Leadership Behavior

The challenges in transforming leadership and organizational behaviors from looking inward to outward are many. And while I can't give you a decoder to all of the situations that exist, there are quite a few reoccurring issues that I experienced in this role, and which most of my clients encounter. We will prepare you for these in this chapter. Once you engage your leaders in some of these, you will be able to continue to advance and customize them for your organization, culture, and leadership team.

To address these more specifically, outlined below are questions and content for each of the three categories of united leadership behavior to support you in engaging your leadership team. Building these actions with them will make your transformation stick.

Unite the Leadership Team

United leadership team prioritization, messaging, and partnership are imperative for employees to observe and experience, so that they can model this behavior among their own peers. The leadership team must be united in how they translate, support, and enable behaviors that earn the right to customer asset growth with consistency.

- **Are we united in how we make decisions that impact customers?**

One of the first activities we often take to unite leaders is using the journey framework to build an operational "code of conduct." Leaders are encouraged to think through tactically, by stage of the experience, what the company must *always* do for customers to honor them and earn the right to growth. Also, by stage of the experience, what should the company *never* do to customers to dishonor them or their time? After this initial effort is worked through with customers and employees, it gives the organization clarity about how to make decisions. It is a powerful first step in embedding the customer journey to inform and enable decision-making.

Most leadership teams don't invest in the deep thinking required to answer these questions. As a result, decisions are driven by silo objectives and inside-out goals and metrics.

Without a conversation uniting leaders in what I call their code of conduct for how they will and will not grow, employees don't have a clear roadmap for how they should steer their decisions. Most important, the decision lens for making decisions varies by leader. This creates confusion, and that confusion results in the random and inconsistent treatment customers receive.

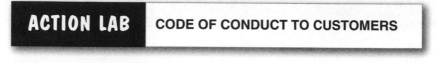

Build your "Code of Conduct" for customer treatment. The following two questions are grounded in using the customer journey framework. As you see, your journey framework serves a great purpose in your transformation, acting as a consistent way to discuss and define priorities and work.

By stage of the customer experience,

What must we **ALWAYS** *do* to honor customers?

What must we **NEVER** *do* to dishonor customers?

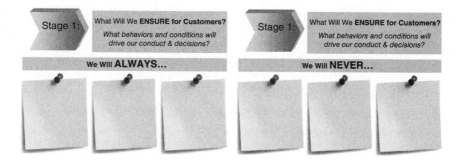

Have this discussion with leaders and engage the organization to establish your code of conduct to guide decision-making to improve customers' lives. Answers to these two questions, when agreed upon, create specificity in operations and behaviors. They unite leaders to be very deliberate about how they will and will not grow. Through communication of these commitments and actions they prove to be a powerful "prove-it" leadership strategy.

"Do This, Don't Do That" Interaction Principles

Ingrid Lindberg
Chief Customer Experience Officer, Prime Therapeutics
Previously, Chief Customer Experience Officer, Cigna

Ingrid Lindberg is Chief Customer Experience Officer at Prime Therapeutics. She was previously Cigna's Customer Experience Officer. Ingrid is responsible for design and implementation of Prime's customer experience strategy, which includes all interactions Prime has with its more than 25 million members, supporting them to get the medicine they need to feel better and live well.

In the course of engaging with leadership teams and organizations in my first 90 days on the job, we conduct a very powerful exercise that moves high-level platitudes into interaction principles for how the company will treat customers.

When mapping the journey stages, we take time to make sure we are stepping through the customers' life to simply list what we will and will not do in each stage. The idea is to make sure that people who participate in this exercise have come already prepped by having read customer feedback by stage of the journey. To keep us grounded in that customer mode, I always have someone in the room also play the role of one of our customers. They are plants in the room to keep us grounded as we identify what we will and won't do.

Next, by stage of the experience, we have people start calling out what you should and should not do for customers. Make sure the actions are explicit, such as "We will never make a customer take more than three steps to talk to a specialist." At the end of this process, which I usually iterate over 90 days with recycling groups, you will have a company-wide set of Interaction Principles. These should guide behaviors, decisions, and prioritization of projects and investments. It is a very smart way to engage the organization while crystallizing the transformation in behavior we are looking to achieve.

• Are we united in focusing on customer asset growth?

The power of competency one, is that it engages leaders in building your version of how you can measure the growth or loss of your customer asset. But it's not enough to just do the math. Leaders must be united in fearlessly talking about the growth or loss of the customer asset at their team meetings. Unity in this messaging is what creates the impact.

Take these actions in unison across the leadership team. When consistently executed and committed to, this messaging has powerful results. It moves the work from being a program and elevates it to the higher purpose of the business.

United Leadership Communication: Focus on Customers as Assets

- *Every* leader starts their meetings with employees by fearlessly sharing the growth or loss of the customer asset in that period.
- Evolve leadership messaging from "getting the score" to "earning the right to customer asset growth."

Put the Voice of the Customer in the Ears of Leaders

- Each month, every leader calls lost customers to care about the "why" behind customer losses, and humanize the life of the customer.
- Tell the story of customers' lives to employees.

Establish One-Company Rewards for Customer Asset Growth

- Evolve to an overall customer experience success metric of company-wide performance in customer asset growth. The measure of customer experience success then becomes your customers voting with their feet to stay or go.

Give Permission and Behaviors to Model

Company dynamics, collaboration, and communication can be effectively addressed, using your customer journey framework as a guide. This is where you address the human issues critical to building your customer growth engine. How are leaders enabling the organization to work? How are decisions made? Why are people rewarded and recognized?

- **Are we united in decisions that enable employees to deliver value?**

Build your code of conduct for how you will support and enable employees by journey stage. Just as you did for customers, follow the process for supporting and enabling employees by journey stage. Be deliberate about what the company will do to honor and enable employees to deliver value, and what it will not do to get in the way.

ACTION LAB   CODE OF CONDUCT TO EMPLOYEES

As part of this process, *ask employees what <u>they</u> need* by customer journey stage. This is a very powerful prove-it action that we use at the beginning of the transformation process. I encourage every leader to actively have these fearless conversations with rotating small groups of employees.

1. By stage of the customer experience, *what must we* ALWAYS *do* to honor employees?
2. By stage of the customer experience, *what must we* NEVER *do* to dishonor employees?

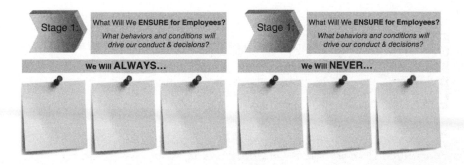

(*continued*)

(*continued*)

These decisions will unite leaders about how they will and will not support employees in enabling customer-driven growth. Communication of these commitments is powerful in proving to employees that the commitment is real.

• Do we kill "stupid rules" that get in the way of employees' delivering value?

Are there rules that get in the way of your employees' ability to deliver value? If there are, they are impeding customer asset growth. Throughout the course of every business, rules are built into the business. Sometimes these made sense when they were established. Sometimes they are created inside the silos, to give them control.

These rules frustrate customers and employees. They cause repeated workaround activities by employees throughout the organization, exhausting them and forcing people to exercise one-off heroics. And they hurt your brand, as only those customers who happen to work with employees who know how to work around clunky rules receive the best experiences.

These rules frustrate employees who repeatedly bring them up to leaders, without seeing them removed. Your employees are put in the position of having to defend practices and rules that they don't agree with, and over time that impacts their belief in the values of the organization and its belief in them.

Would You Treat Your Mother This Way?

Dan Pastoric
Executive Vice President & Chief Customer Officer
Enersource

Dan Pastoric is Executive Vice President and Chief Customer Officer at Enersource Corporation in Ontario, Canada, where he is leading corporate strategy, increasing shareholder value in both the regulated and non-regulated businesses. He manages all customer-care service functions including Conservation and Demand Management.

Most organizations believe they have purged all the dumb rules and over the past few years we have worked hard to be more efficient and much more responsive. A policy review is carried out each year to ensure that our rules, policies, or procedures are kept up to date with changing technology, business philosophies, and customer trends.

The question we keep in mind as we review each of them is, "Does this policy still fit with our changing culture?" Being in a regulated industry, regulators provide direction of what they believe the consumer wants or needs, and sometimes those rules or directions seem to be layered on and on again, putting greater constraints on the business. We see the impact of those directives and are working to make changes, to syphon off the inefficient and impractical rules. To that end, our executive team is very engaged in this process and has gone through and streamlined their operations, considering the interconnection and our ability to support the enterprise versus our individual business units. We are across the board working to minimize the number of procedures to get something done.

For our people, we try to make this less structured and more cultural. We say to them, "If this (customer) was your mother or a relative of yours in this situation, would you treat them this way?" Would you make a decision to put a utility pole in the middle of their front yard? Would you return their call right away? We are encouraging our team, front line to executive, to be more connected to our customers in an intelligent and very human way in everything they do, from giving out information, acting as their advocates, or taking action. By asking them to make decisions through the lens of how they would treat their own mom, they can personally contact with the customer. They own the process and are engaged in the situation.

ACTION LAB   KILL A STUPID RULE MOVEMENT

I have mentioned killing stupid rules before, but this tactic has become so successful with clients that it merits its own Action Lab. This is one of the most fast-moving and effective prove-it actions you can take—especially early in your company's transformation. When you improve employees' lives they will improve customers' lives. Leadership teams must be united in killing stupid rules and rewarding employees who fearlessly bring up these rules.

(continued)

(*continued*)

> ### "KILL A STUPID RULE" MOVEMENT
>
> Create a "Kill a Stupid Rule" movement,
> encouraging employees to identify rules that
> erode customer trust and diminish employee's
> ability to do their job.
>
> Reward for the identification of rules that just
> don't make sense. Then kill those rules!
> Let employees know you
> took action.
> (market hope)

- **Do we enable cross-silo experience understanding and action?**

As outlined in Competency 3, Build a Customer Listening Path, information from multiple sources tells the true story of your customers' lives. As you unite as a leadership team, there must be a commitment to not be reactive to survey results or anecdotal one-off information to drive silo-based actions.

Build a customer listening path using multiple sources of customer input. Emancipate your dependency on survey results by combining volunteer (unaided) feedback, behavioral experiences, operational performance, and aided (survey) feedback to tell the story of your customers' lives. Transition presentations from silo or survey question dashboards to present collective information from multiple sources—along the path of your customer journey.

- **Do we practice capacity creation? Or do we layer on projects without taking anything off the list?**

Without managing the workload of company members who will be engaged in customer experience transformation activities, leaders can't prove commitment. Layering customer work on top of the already full plates of operational leaders and teams is the recipe for customer focus abandonment. Yet that is what I encounter with every client as we do this work. The question "Do you have a stop-doing list?" is met with nervous laughter. Exhausted employees will agree with the importance, but the "can't get there from here" perception will impede the work.

ACTION LAB INTELLIGENT STOP-DOING LIST

Build an intelligent "stop-doing" list. Use your customer journey framework to inventory all of the current projects from every operating area tagged to improve customer experiences. List them under each stage of the experience they would impact when implemented.

This exercise will assist in identifying duplicate projects focused on the same customer experiences from within multiple silos. By examining projects and stacking them in this manner across the journey, you can determine how well resources are being allocated to improve complete customer experiences, or if your inventory represents silo-based splinter projects driven by silo objectives.

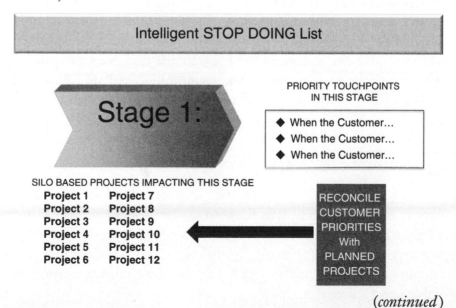

Intelligent STOP DOING List

Stage 1:

PRIORITY TOUCHPOINTS
IN THIS STAGE

◆ When the Customer...
◆ When the Customer...
◆ When the Customer...

SILO BASED PROJECTS IMPACTING THIS STAGE

Project 1	Project 7
Project 2	Project 8
Project 3	Project 9
Project 4	Project 10
Project 5	Project 11
Project 6	Project 12

RECONCILE CUSTOMER PRIORITIES With PLANNED PROJECTS

(*continued*)

(*continued*)

CEOs and leadership teams get a false-positive on the level of customer-centric change being executed because multitudes of projects with "customer" show up in annual planning, budgeting, and presentations.

Use the customer journey framework to inventory projects and make decisions on how to create capacity at the beginning of this work. Then, continue its use to give you a comprehensive view of workload, capacity, and commitment required to enable future work. The ongoing use of your customer journey framework will reinforce the commitment to delivering a one-company experience to the organization. A commitment that must start with capacity creation.

Prove It with Action

The leadership team must be united in the actions that they invest in. This means that leaders are united in how they assess and prioritize investment to earn customer-driven growth. The organization needs to see that every leader is not translating and acting independently but rather that they are connected as a team. Leadership language and explanations of these priorities must be unison. As these decisions are made, employees need to be apprised of them, with the reasoning behind why the decisions and investments were made. It is these explicit examples of collaboration and customer-driven decision-making that give people permission to model the same behaviors in their operations and roles.

- **Do we drive regular accountability?**

The way that most customer conversations are held is a report out on project plans focused on improving survey scores or showing a project plan with red-yellow-green dots. This does not engage leaders; as many of my clients say, "People just sort of tune out during my report." Yet the sales conversations are robust and spirited.

My recommendation is to build a customer room. Using the customer room to drive monthly, quarterly, and annual accountability is one of the most robust actions that we use to align leaders and drive customer-driven action. It engages leaders personally in customers' lives and unites them to make decisions. It establishes an accountability forum that transcends most governance meetings on the subject, where projects are reported but engaging in understanding and improving customers' lives is not always built-in.

ACTION LAB	**BUILD A CUSTOMER ROOM**

The customer room is a tangible depiction of your customers' journey with you. It is where storytelling is enabled as the output from each of the five competencies comes together to tell the story of your customers' lives.

The power of the customer room is the visual storytelling. That is because it is set up as an experience—a way for your leaders and organization to step through customers' lives.

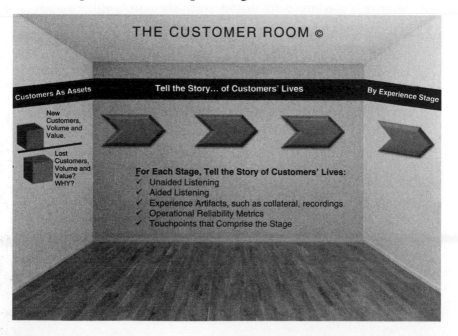

THE CUSTOMER ROOM ©

Customers As Assets   Tell the Story... of Customers' Lives   By Experience Stage

New Customers, Volume and Value.

Lost Customers, Volume and Value? WHY?

For Each Stage, Tell the Story of Customers' Lives:
- Unaided Listening
- Aided Listening
- Experience Artifacts, such as collateral, recordings
- Operational Reliability Metrics
- Touchpoints that Comprise the Stage

Here is the power of engaging leaders regularly in the customer room.

- *Connects the Work to ROI.* Ask, "Did we earn the right to customer growth?" This is where you present the visual depiction of customer as assets—the outcome of the growth or loss of your customers and their few key behavioral actions showing growth or diminishment of engagement and bond. This is where leaders prove that they care about the "why" behind whether customers stayed or left.

- **Breeds *Caring about Customers' Lives.*** Create empathy for your customers. Do this by walking through the current experience to know what customers are going through. By stage of the experience, show the story visually with what they experience, what they hear, and how customers react. Here you assemble information built from multiple sources of listening organized by stage of the customer experience. Make this active and visual by also showing screenshots, the paperwork customers have to fill out, and videos, and playing recorded calls—make executives try to do what you require customers to do so they step through the life of the customer.

- **Unites *Focus, Prioritization, and Commitments.*** Unite leaders to select experiences for improvement or innovation. Once you walk through the stages of the customer experience and identify emerging priorities, leaders collectively and in a united manner select which experiences they will add as priorities to be addressed. This establishes focus on the critical few versus the many silo-based projects that come out of a "customer experience" focus sent out to the organization to independently interpret and begin acting upon.

- *Drives Accountability and Reward the Middle.* Get rid of volunteer fatigue. We have exhausted the middle of nearly every organization I work with due to the volunteer task forces that are assembled to work on customer experiences. This is usually done alongside every other special project that has been layered onto what has already been planned for the year. Instead establish a reliable cycle of accountability for the teams you task to improve customer experiences. Use your customer room to have the teams report back each month following this simple path:

- Month 1: Current customer experience for the selected experience.
- Month 2: Identify root cause issues and current measures.
- Month 3: Recommendations for actions and budget.
- Month 4: Begin actions.
- When complaints previously trended on the issue start to decline, reward the team.

Please consider this is a straw man, as this cycle should be accelerated or lengthened depending on the complexity of the customer issue or experience redesign. The power here is the clear path given to leaders for selecting focus areas and the path given to assembled teams assigned to tackling them. The customer room experience provides your leadership team with rigor for driving accountability and embeds the competency of a customer experience development (CXD) process as outlined in Competency 4: Experience Reliability and Innovation. Many times teams tackling customer experiences are assembled without proper leadership advocacy and alignment at the initiation of the work. As a result, they feel like beggars seeking the attention, resource, and commitment from leaders for their actions (usually layered on their regular work load). The customer room process, when continued as a regular part of leaders' commitment to customer-driven growth, energizes both leadership and the organization and continues the momentum required for transformation.

Building Our Customer Room

Michael Bennett
Senior Vice President, Operations
The Irvine Company

Mike Bennett is Senior Vice President, Operations for the Irvine Company Office Properties, where he leads a customer-driven transformational effort with the leadership team that began in 2010 and continues today. Irvine Company Office Properties manages a portfolio of 500 office and industrial properties throughout California.

We built out our customer room for a combination of reasons. It plays a role as war room where we work as a team to focus on our customer experience challenges and present ideas to leadership for improvement, and it plays a key role in how we onboard new employees and exemplify our culture around the customer. It is also a place where we recognize achievement for individuals, teams, and our overall key customer loyalty metrics.

In our customer room, we have posted each stage of the customer experience on the walls so we can identify issues and opportunities. Here we tack up comments, letters, and screen shots of web pages that we are improving. Across each stage we highlight priorities we are working on to improve touch-point processes and experiences. Teams work in this room cross-functionally on a regular basis as we identify priorities. Although the focus is on internal processes, customers, consultants, and service partners who visit can see the improvement efforts that we are currently focusing on.

We are also using our customer room as a cultural space to onboard new employees. When we talked with customers and coworkers as we built out our customer journey and priorities, we learned that our onboarding of employees and customers was widely varied. We wanted to have a more robust initial experience so we came up with a very interactive experience for our new employees. On day one this includes a bus tour of our asset properties with interaction from different leaders at each property. The day ends at our headquarters in our customer room where one or more selected leaders meet face-to-face and learn cultural and company information about our efforts to put employees and customers at the center of our business.

Another important dimension of our customer room is its use for recognition. A big screen is in the middle of the room, facing visitors when they enter. Here we post quotes, key statistics, and metrics illustrating how we are improving our customers' experiences and meeting our key financial results. Teams are also recognized within this space to celebrate hard work being done throughout the company. It's a celebration space and a concept we are talking about duplicating in our field offices.

This room is having an impact because (a) it is indoctrinating our new employees to our customer-centric culture during orientation, (b) it is enhancing creativity within our teams, encouraging them to work together to impact customer growth, and (c) other Irvine Company divisions are seeking our assistance to help them set up their own rooms.

- **Do our decisions match our commitment? Do we tell employees?**

Do you live up to your "Code of Conduct?" Your employees need to see decisions that are congruent to your commitment to improving customer experiences. The power of establishing a united customer journey is that it provides a customer-driven framework for decision-making and communication back to the organization.

Market Hope. As you make decisions in alignment with your commitment to improving customers' lives, employees need to know these decisions and the intent behind them. This communication provides ongoing clarity on actions that they can model.

As you provide examples for people to emulate, use the customer journey to show where customers' lives were improved, recognizing the multiple silos whose collaboration was required to deliver a complete experience.

- **Does annual planning begin by examining customers' lives?**

Over the years I've become convinced that annual planning is the Achilles' heel of customer experience. Annual planning is at the root of what inhibits the most efficient investment on priority investments in customer driven growth. That is because annual planning starts with the silos, not the customer asset, and not the customer journey. As a result, the customer experience becomes the defaulted outcome of every silo's budget and projects they plan to spend that money.

ACTION LAB | RETHINK ANNUAL PLANNING

As companies go through the planning cycle, there should be a decision-making framework to guide investment on customer experiences most critical for customer-driven growth. Often there is not. Clarity for corporate-led investments such as data, infrastructure, and so forth are now being addressed with a more disciplined approach at the enterprise level. But investments and actions focused on customer experiences remain, for the most part, silo driven.

Do You Capitalize on Annual Planning to Manage Customers as Assets?

Annual planning is a missed opportunity for driving customer growth. Without a one-company review of growth or loss of the customer asset and a diagnosis of the experience impacts, the company continues to focus only on business outcomes. And companies continue to stand still regarding customer asset growth without knowing exactly why.

Annual planning of customer-centered goals should include:

- Customer asset current state analysis: Volume and value of lost customers and volume and value of new customers required to drive incremental growth.
- Identifying priority customer experiences driving customers out the door.
- Goals for customer movement from one level of engagement to the next.

Start annual planning with your version of the customer room. Have the leadership team thoroughly understand the growth or loss of the customer asset. Use the customer room to diagnose and understand the "why?" behind customer asset growth or loss: how the experience aided or impeded growth. Then use this process to identify experiences most critical to diminish customer losses, improve reliability, or innovate experiences to differentiate your company to customers and partners. Establish a clear communication plan and roadmap for the organization on the top five to ten priorities that emerge.

Communicate the outcome of the customer-room decision making sessions, identifying customer priorities across the customer journey. Determine corporate-level resource requirements to solve the complete customer experience. *Then*, allocate the funds back to the silos. Or, as some clients do, keep these funds at the corporate level to ensure their preservation.

This change to annual planning prioritization from the customer journey perspective versus traditional silo-based planning will drive culture change, and will advance your commitment to customer-driven growth.

(continued)

(continued)

Finally, don't declare that *this* is the year of the customer. Make the messaging and the action operationally relevant by being clear about which part of the experience needs focus and commitment and why. This very operational and tangible approach is very potent. It is a clear prove-it action that aligns leaders and the organization.

Storytelling Works Better than Charts

Hilary Noon
Vice President, Marketplace Insight and Experience
The American Cancer Society

Hilary Noon is Vice President of Marketplace Insight and Experience at the American Cancer Society. In her role she is the thought leader responsible for driving customer-focused strategy at the C-suite and business-unit-owner levels of the organization.

We have learned that how we present information is just as important if not more so than what we present. People are much more likely to understand and internalize information when our presentations are visual and engaging. We therefore use a storytelling methodology instead of producing heavy reports with tons of data. Emphasis is on the use of visuals to create a theme and unite the findings from all the critical data sources.

We have also learned to customize the messaging to the audience. For example, for our younger volunteers and staff who are responsible for executing our events, we leverage visuals to a greater degree and bring in some humor using pop-culture references to generate stickiness and greater appeal. These often take the form of customized one-pagers highlighting what they need to focus on most. We also customize the output to incorporate the visual look and feel of the event including specific use of color, pictures, and brand.

Even with senior leadership we use visual storytelling to catch their attention and direct it to the areas of highest impact. This typically involves a lot less text and more focus on the key headlines. With this audience in particular, we have to balance the desire to make the information visually appealing with the need to communicate confidence that the data and methodology is sound and that they can trust the results.

A key goal with our work is to make the message digestible, so that the need to prioritize the donor and constituent experience is not only promoted by our team but is embraced and shared by other leaders. This is achieved through partnership at the leadership level and by enabling the staff on the front line to consume the information and put it into practice. By encouraging leaders to own the information about their donors and key constituents we have observed that that they put a greater emphasis on the experience at both a strategic and tactical level.

Competency Five Impact When Implemented

Over time, it will become clear that the work of your company is to earn the right to growth by improving customers' lives. Leadership plans, investments, and the order of how products are built, services are established, and people are supported will be guided by the commitment to honor and grow customers as assets. Actions will prove that a united leadership team is deliberately steering the company in the direction of supporting customers' lives.

That will be *then*. This is *now*. Don't despair.

The key to this work is breaking it into achievable actions. That is why throughout this book, you have been provided with tactics and "recipe cards" at the end of each competency chapter. This work most successfully begins with creating simple and clear behaviors for leaders, the middle of the organization and the frontline on how to unite their efforts.

Establish how you will hire people who have values congruent with your company core values. Enable the frontline by removing rules and roadblocks that inhibit their ability to deliver value by stage of the customer journey. Get rid of the roadblocks that most often require work-around solutions, exhaust employees, and force them to rework every issue in order to serve customers. Remove policies or rules incongruent to a commitment for improving customers' lives. For those in functional roles, challenge and reward them for working together across their silos to improve complete customer experiences.

Then commit to these behaviors. Embed them as part of the business engine, as a consistent component in how every leader leads across the organization. These behaviors are not a program. Not a work stream. People inside your company will only believe this is real and start taking actions (without explicit scorecard mandates) when they experience proof in consistent and enduring one-company leadership behavior.

Customer-Driven Growth Inhibitors

Before we end this chapter, I want to summarize the *inverse* of embedding competencies as part of your transformation effort. These are inhibitors that most companies encounter as they embark on this work in one form or another. They stand in the way of improving customers' lives and earning the right to growth.

The five customer leadership competencies in this book have been developed and field-tested to help you avoid and reduce the impact of each of these inhibitors. They link together to build your customer-driven growth engine.

7 Inhibitors to Customer-Driven Growth.

1. Not having executives engaged in the effort.

2. Starting with a mantra, not an action plan.

3. Not defining the Customer experience & gaining alignment.

4. Not breaking the work into actionable pieces.

5. Focusing first on survey scores and not customer growth.

6. Lack of clear communication and behaviors to model.

7. Actions based on what people think vs. what Customers.

1. **Not having executives engaged in the effort.** As you saw in the build-out of these competencies, there is an operational and a behavioral element to each one. Often executives will say that they want to focus on the customer experience, but they hand off the tasks to a department or area to work on it. This work is not like a typical project. Setting up a great project plan and executing on tactics and actions will get the infrastructure built (such as VOC systems), but it won't drive the change in culture and the development of cross-silo competencies. It is hard to sustain this work without executive involvement driving the new prioritization, removing actions that are in the way, and giving people permission to work together.

2. **Starting with a mantra, not an action plan.** Often companies decide that they want to get some early traction by telling everyone to "focus on customer experience." What happens next is that people realize this is a big corporate priority and begin making plans, creating new scoreboards and taking action. This advances the silo-based approach to actions that are contrary to the discipline of experience development and management. A lot of action occurs, executives get a false-positive that change is occurring, but it eventually stalls out because the actions don't add up to improve complete end-to-end customer experiences.

Have a specific three-month, six-month and twelve-month plan ready to go when you launch. Explicitly identify the process for collaboration and roles. Every month, just like the map in the shopping centers, send an update showing "we are here"—pointing to progress made. Continue to communicate the plan as it progresses and adjusts.

3. **Not defining the customer experience and gaining alignment.** The *most potent* recurring use for the journey map is to guide work and discussions from the customer perspective. Without this framework to unite efforts, silo work continues to proliferate.

Here are a few reasons why agreement on the stages of the experience and the definitions of success are important:

(a) it gives leaders a new language set for asking questions and guiding the business, (b) it establishes the critical cross-functional metrics for the development of key performance indicators (KPIs) for priority touch points, and (c) it aligns big data and database management (since the stages of the experience interrelate to one another).

4. **Not breaking the work into actionable pieces.** Don't boil the ocean. Successful CCOs advocate prioritizing five to ten (at most) priorities at a time. Following through until they are completely implemented will earn the right to keep doing the work. Making this work too large is why it fails. Over time this will become part of the work of the operation, but for some time, it will appear as layered-on work. You need to accomplish something, then market it back, learn, and continue forward.

5. **Focusing only on survey scores and not on customer growth.** The challenge of focusing mostly on survey scores is that the score is the motivator. And, a survey score is impacted by numerous factors, not all of which can be impacted by areas of the organization that are given the outcome metrics as their performance score. Focus on the growth or loss of the customer asset, the highest level of customer experience performance. In addition, identify operational metrics that people can impact—such as operational KPIs (instead of getting attached to early outcome survey scores).

If survey metrics are added too early to compensation, before the underlying processes—culture change, coaching, and development—are put into place, people *will* want to get good scores, but they will bypass the work that earns the score, and … sometimes lean on customers to get a better score. ("Any reason you can't give me a 10?") They will also focus on actions so minute that they might move the needle a little on the score, but the overall approach to sustaining that skill or even building that skill is compromised. It's very hard to sustain the go-get-a-good-score approach.

6. **Lack of clear communications and behaviors to model.** It's not enough to do the work behind the scenes:

the organization must be kept up to speed on actions, what it means to them, and successes. Leaders must emerge as constant communicators of why we are taking the actions we are. As new decisions are made that focus on customer experiences—people must be kept apprised of these decisions—and given permission to model this type of decision-making. Without this constant communication, permission setting, and decision guidance the organization will view customer experience work as another project in a long string of exercises or programs that will go the way of the others—away.

7. **Actions based on what people think versus what customers need.** Many companies, especially those long entrenched in their business, believe they know what customers need. Even when they do research, they make the research about "validating" their plans rather than beginning by being open-minded and asking the customer about their lives and what they need. This approach often compromises the outcome of new experiences invested in—and in some cases will backfire as the investment yields negative customer response.

How We Got Traction...

Mary Poppen
Chief Customer Officer
SAP, Global Cloud Business

Mary Poppen is Chief Customer Officer at SAP, Global Cloud Business. She is responsible for the definition, measurement, and improvement of the total customer experience, including engagement, value and adoption, research, and operational transformation, across SAP Cloud lines of business.

As our survey results came in, it was hard, as in most companies, to gain alignment and ownership for solving problems. We were talking among ourselves and not making great traction. Everyone was looking at results through the lens of their own silo. So we decided to neutralize how and what we were hearing by having an outside team interview our customers, our partners, and our internal people.

(continued)

(*continued*)

What they identified correlated a good deal with what we had presented in our data, but this time the message resonated, because:

- It was the customer's spoken feedback.
- A third party presented the real challenges rather than debating them among ourselves.
- The findings were broken into specific operational issues.

To not boil the ocean in response to these findings, we chose 12 clear operational actions that our customers outlined as important. We organized these actions into five pillars including Product, Operations, Implementation, Enablement, and Support. After our senior leadership team acknowledged the issues and agreed on the priorities, we introduced the commitments to customers at our annual user conferences. We knew that if we committed publicly to customers, we had to deliver.

From this approach, we moved from verbal commitments and debating survey scores to action. For example, we had been talking for two years about separating our test and production customer environments. Customers wanted to preview new functionality to prepare for how best to leverage it within their live system. We had discussed this request a lot, but never acted on it. We are now starting a waved approach of bringing this enhancement, along with several other commitments, to customers as a result of cross-functional alignment focused on making customer feedback human and operational.

ACTION LAB   LEADERSHIP BEHAVIORS

Below is a summary of key behaviors for Competency 5: Leadership, Accountability, and Culture, which will prove commitment with united messaging and actions. This is important: don't take these on all at once. Stair-step them and gain agreement from your leadership team, then don't stop once you start.

Leadership Behaviors to Drive Transformation

Competency 5: Leadership, Accountability, and Culture

Align the Leadership Team

Tell the Story of Your Customers' Lives

Build a customer room to unite the leadership team in regularly traversing the customer journey to identify opportunities and priorities.

Use the customer room as an onboarding and orientation experience for new hires.

Give Permission

Establish Regular Accountability

Convene C-suite monthly, quarterly, and annually to understand customers' lives, and drive focus and accountability.

Unite Prioritization & Capacity Creation:

Intelligent capacity creation. Use the customer journey to inventory projects and establish a "stop doing" list.

Prove It with Action

Revise Annual Planning to Start with Customers' Lives and Customer Asset Growth.

Revise annual planning to be guided by a one-company review of the customer experience to determine priorities and and investments.

Market Hope.

Communicate rigorously with employees on actions, decisions, priorities, and the evolving customer and employee journey.

ACTION LAB   **LEADERSHIP TRANSFORMATION PLAN**

Your Leadership Transformation Plan

In this book you've been introduced to the five competencies chapter by chapter. To assist you in your company's transformation I've assembled the leadership actions that are recommended for each of the five competencies into this comprehensive list. You can use this list to work with your leaders to engage them in "proving it" to your organization that they are committed to earning the right to customer-driven growth.

LEADERSHIP BEHAVIORS TO DRIVE TRANSFORMATION

Competency 1: Honor and Manage Customers As Assets

Know the Growth and Loss of Customers and Care about the "Why?"

With this competency, the purpose is to shift to a simple understanding and measurement of success when a company achieves customer-driven growth. Customer asset metrics track *what customers actually did* versus translating (and debating) what they *say they might do* via survey results. Leaders must start taking it personally that customers are departing from their business. They need to care about the math between customers in and customers out—because that delta drives growth. They need to make the connection between customer experience improvement and the movement of these metrics. Customer asset metrics create a way for executives to know and care about the shifting behavior within your customer base, which indicates whether customers' bond with your company is growing or shrinking.

ALIGN THE LEADERSHIP TEAM

United Messaging: Focus on Customer Asset Growth

✓ Every leader starts their meetings with employees by fearlessly sharing the growth or loss of the customer asset.

✓ Evolve leadership messaging from "getting the score" to "earning the right" to customer growth.

GIVE PERMISSION

Enable People to Growth the Customer Asset

✓ Create a "Kill a Stupid Rule" movement, encouraging employees to identify rules that erode customer trust and diminish employee ability to do their job and deliver value.

✓ Reward people who identify rules that just don't make sense. And kill those rules! Let employees know when they've been eliminated.

PROVE IT WITH ACTION

Put the Voice of the Customer in Your Ear

✓ Every month call lost customers—to demonstrate caring for why customers stay or go, and humanize customers for leaders. Tell stories of customers' lives to employees.

(continued)

(continued)

Reward for Customer Asset Growth

✓ Move your overall customer-centric success metric from survey scores to overall performance in customer asset growth—the true measure of your customer experience.

Competency 2: Align around Experience

Give Leaders a Framework for Guiding the Work of the Organization
Unite Accountability as Customers Experience You, Not Down Your Silos

A journey framework, even in its simplest form, when used with consistency provides rigor to understand priorities in customers' lives. Evaluating and understanding the entire customer journey enables leaders to make choices. This moves the work from boiling the ocean, trying to drive improvement on all the touch points to *focusing* on those that impact customer-driven growth. This establishes a framework for leaders to use communicating the business purpose, and how they drive accountability across the enterprise to improve customers' lives.

ALIGN THE LEADERSHIP TEAM

United Leadership Alignment on the Customer Journey

✓ Leaders align on the stages of your customer experience and prioritized 10 to 15 key touch points.
✓ Change in leadership language and accountability goes from silo report out to driving accountability by experience stage.

GIVE PERMISSION

Drive Accountability and Enable Performance by Customer Experience Stage

✓ Leaders regularly engage with the frontline and behind the scenes to discuss, by stage, what is hindering their work. What is impacting customers?

✓ Develop hiring and development tools and support for employees to deliver value by stage of the experience.

PROVE IT WITH ACTION

United Leadership Decision-Making Code of Conduct

✓ Unite leaders to agree by stage of the experience: What will you always do to honor customers and/or employees? What will you never do to dishonor, disappoint, or distrust them?

Communicate and Reward Decisions

✓ Free employees to make decisions guided by your code of conduct, defining what you must always do and never do by experience stage. Reward for decisions made.

Competency 3: Build a Customer Listening Path

Seek Input and Customer Understanding, Aligned to the Customer Journey

Your customer listening path will unite leaders and the organization in understanding experiences impacting customer growth or loss. Through stepping leaders and the organization experientially through the customer journey, *improving customers' lives to earn the right to growth motivates actions.* Storytelling using multiple sources of information and visual and experiential learning drives actions to improve unreliable experiences and uncover innovation opportunity. As you build out your listening path, your customer journey provides the frame for storytelling. Those stages allow you to collapse multiple sources of information, such as feedback volunteered from customers as they interact with you, survey feedback, social feedback, experiential listening, and other research to tell the one-company story of customer interactions with you across their journey.

ALIGN THE LEADERSHIP TEAM

Leaders Commit to a United One-Company Listening Path

✓ Gain agreement to build a one-company customer listening path across the enterprise.

✓ Combine multiple sources of listening to show patterns of customer need and value growth or erosion. Move the emphasis from the score to understanding and improving customers' lives to earn the right to growth.

GIVE PERMISSION

Enable Cross-Silo Experience Understanding and Action

✓ Transition presentation of customer listening content from survey or silo-based dashboard to insights by stage of the customer journey.

✓ Advocate cross-company collaboration to improve the experience, not try to just get lift on a survey score.

PROVE IT WITH ACTION

Practice Active and "Experiential" Listening:
Walk in the Customers' Shoes

✓ You need to know the life to serve the life. Be a customer. Identify the actions you require customers to take in key touch points across the journey. Stage timing for leaders to take those actions themselves.

Walk the Talk

✓ Stop reactive one-off projects and fire drills started from anecdotal or incomplete, silo-based information.

Competency 4: Proactive Experience Reliability and Innovation

Know before Customers Tell You Where Experiences Are Unreliable
Build your "Revenue Erosion Early Warning" System

Competency four builds your "Revenue Erosion Early Warning System." It enables your leaders to know *before customers tell you* if your operation is reliable in performing at key customer intersection points. To drive customer asset growth, leaders need to care about and require reliable operational performance in key customer intersection points. These intersection points along your customer journey impact customers' evaluation of value delivered. They drive decisions to stay, leave, buy more, and recommend you to others. To earn the right to customer asset growth, they require consistency in how they are executed across the channels, the silos, and your business.

ALIGN THE LEADERSHIP

Require Operational Performance That Earns Customer Growth

✓ Leaders require accountability in key customer experiences to equal their rigor in demanding sales performance.

✓ Make customer experience development (CXD) a core competency as critical as product development.

GIVE PERMISSION

Commit Resources to Customer Experience Development

✓ Build the competency of a cross-silo customer experience development process—CXD.

✓ Provide resources for cross-functional teams to work together to improve and innovate experiences, processes, and metrics that drive value and earn customer growth.

PROVE IT WITH ACTION

Give Customer Experience Development Time to Embed into the Business Engine

✓ Allow the customer experience development process the time and resources necessary for it to become a competency of the business. Don't abandon it because it takes time.

> ### Reward Cross-Silo Collaboration
> ✓ Reward cross-company teams for complaint reduction and for sustainable experience improvement.

Competency 5: Leadership, Accountability, and Culture

*Leadership Behaviors required for Embedding the Five Competencies
Enabling Employees to Deliver Value*

This is your prove-it-to-me competency. For this work to be transformative and stick, it must be more than a customer manifesto. Commitment to customer-driven growth is proven with action and choices. To emulate culture, people need examples. They need proof. Competency five is the glue that holds the customer-driven growth engine together. It puts into practice leadership behaviors required by a united leadership team to enable customer asset growth.

ALIGN THE LEADERSHIP TEAM

> ### Tell the Story of Customers' Lives
> ✓ Build a customer room to unite the leadership team in regularly traversing the customer journey to identify opportunities and priorities.
> ✓ Use the customer room as an onboarding and orientation experience for new hires.

GIVE PERMISSION

Establish Regular Accountability

✓ Convene the customer room monthly, quarterly, and annually to drive regular accountability as a leadership team and across silo teams.

✓ Use the customer room as the forum for experience improvement accountability.

Prioritization and Capacity Creation

✓ Practice intelligent capacity creation. Use the customer journey to inventory projects and establish a stop-doing list.

✓ When new projects are established, practice rigor in managing capacity and trade-offs.

PROVE IT WITH ACTION

Embed Customer Room Accountability into Your Business Engine

✓ Revise annual planning to be guided by a one-company review of the customer experience to determine key focused priorities and investments.

Market Hope

✓ Communicate rigorously with employees on actions, decisions, priorities, and the evolving customer and employee journey.

Staging the Work

In this chapter we'll address how to break the work of the five competencies into actionable and attainable segments. We will also tackle the ever-popular question of timing, usually worded as "How fast can we get this done?" My goal here is to give you a clear and practical roadmap to get on with it. The three categories addressed in this chapter are:

- Five-Competency Maturity Map and Milestones
- Evolving Organizational Structures
- Chief Customer Officer Priorities by Year

This work will be successful when you take a stair-stepped approach to gaining leadership clarity and commitment to the framework and actions. As you embed the five competencies over time, what you stand for as a company will shift. Starting with the lives of customers and employees will drive decision-making and elevate how you are perceived.

Five Competency Maturity Map

How the Five Competencies Mature over Time to Build Your Customer-Driven Growth Engine

Below is a maturity map for the five customer leadership competencies. For each phase of the Maturity Map, I've identified actions and behavior changes along the continuum of years one through five as the competencies are being embedded. After year five, it is a matter of sharpening and improving these competencies for your organization. By their very nature, the five competencies are not a program, but rather a repeated cycle of one-company awareness, understanding, focus, and united action. We are finding that the five competencies begin to feel embedded and truly repeatable in the third year. I haven't assigned each of these stages by year, but rather by outcome, as timing for moving across the maturity map will vary by organization.

Five Competencies Maturity Map
How Customer Experience Matures Over Time

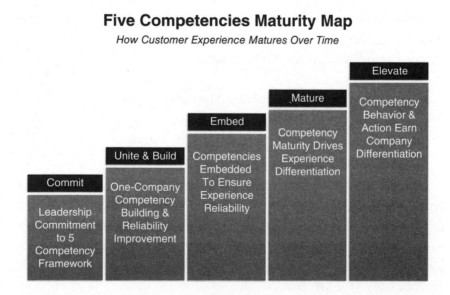

Commit — Leadership Commitment to 5 Competency Framework

Unite & Build — One-Company Competency Building & Reliability Improvement

Embed — Competencies Embedded To Ensure Experience Reliability

Mature — Competency Maturity Drives Experience Differentiation

Elevate — Competency Behavior & Action Earn Company Differentiation

Commit

Gain leadership clarity and commitment to the five-competency framework: to your transformation strategy. This work hinges on *clarity*. Executives need to understand *specifically*, what work is ahead, in terms of both company actions and their actions, decision-making, and behaviors.

The five competencies framework provides that clarity for describing the work ahead to them. To that end, please use the examples in this book and the explanations for each to ensure that leadership team is united in understanding and accepting the scope of work. Most important, ensure that they can stand behind the strategy of the five-competencies framework, or other strategy as you begin the work. If your leadership team when fully apprised of the scope of the work and their required involvement still wants to advance the work, then proceed.

Staging Work to Embed Speed, Agility, & CX Design

Heather Carroll Cox
Chief Client Experience, Digital and Marketing Officer
Citi

Heather Carroll Cox is Chief Client Experience, Digital and Marketing Officer, at Citi where she is responsible for the vision, strategy, structure, and execution of a common client experience, driving global NPS efforts and leading digital, marketing, and decision management across global consumer banking.

As I began in this role, investing in relationships was, and continues to be, my number-one priority in making this work successful. Without it, you are a CCO standing on an island by yourself submitting reports and hoping people will pay attention.

As I am building relationships, I also am working swiftly to define a vision that people can feel and know we can execute against. This has meant pushing up against how we usually plan and get things done. Like many big companies we tend to like big, monolithic programs.

(continued)

(*continued*)

We plan for them, button them down, put them into a long development cycle, and then send them to the marketplace.

For example, we kicked off work in early 2014 to deliver remarkable client experiences that reached across the organization, involving many volunteer participants. While the work was great, we quickly learned it was so large in scale that it might have been two years before outcomes reached customers. We decided to hit the pause button to educate the organization in customer experience transformation skills and agility.

We converted the work to bite-sized chunks. We swiftly moved in 30- to 90-day sprints with ideating, building, and testing new ideas. Taking a page from lean processes and start-up companies, the goal was to take small, bite-size actions without fear of failure. We needed to build open-mindedness to agility and speed—and to the fact that this approach was high risk, but high reward when it hit...

We have built small agile teams with dedicated, high-performance people to accomplish this remarkable client experience work. To build these teams, we are assembling our internal high performers along with best-of-breed external consultants. We've isolated them as focused, full-time teams to start breaking the moments that matter along the client journey down into bite-size pieces. We've also had to embed experience design thinking and competency throughout. It is key and core to everything we do, and it is working. We will have our first efforts out this June in multiple markets across the United States, Asia, Europe, and Latin America.

Unite and Build

Unite leaders and the organization to begin competency building and your first round of experience reliability improvements. In this phase, two outcomes are important: initiating the build of your five-competency engine and taking actions that focus on and improve priority experiences. Think of this as your beta version of this work. First, initiating your five-competency engine means to begin the process of building your first clunky version of each competency. Don't get caught up in the trap that they must be perfect in order to get started.

For example, when you start building your first version of customer asset metrics, all the data may not be perfectly lined up or organized. Establish your first version of the growth or loss of your customer asset and key customer behaviors to watch—*using the data you now have*. The key is to begin. Then evolve from there. Don't wait until the systems are all perfect. We almost always have to start asset metrics with at least partial manual manipulation of data.

As you acquaint yourself with each of these five competencies and begin to customize them for your organization, do what makes sense in each to begin. Take a look at the section below entitled "First Action Milestones," which will assist you in breaking the work into achievable pieces to ensure success and completion. Remember that the organization needs to be engaged and communicated with as you work through these competencies so that over time, the cycle of these five competencies is embedded into your operational business engine.

Focus on bringing experience reliability to a few priority touchpoints. Most chief customer officers agree that it's smart to focus on no more than three to five priorities at a time. Learn the tools to improve customer experience reliability as outlined in Competency 4, Proactive Experience Reliability and Innovation. Then begin to use them as a repeatable process for improving your first set of priority customer touchpoints.

Product-driven companies, for example, have a clear path for product development, improvement and innovation with steps that are clearly understood and followed. In these early days, you begin to build the equivalent of this process for customer experience improvement and innovation. To borrow a phrase that a few of my clients have used, the goal over time is to make customer experience development (CXD) as important as new product development (NPD).

Embed

At this stage, the competencies are now part of how you do work inside your company. By this stage your leadership team should be united in driving accountability by customer journey stage, rather than silo-by-silo. Because they have now been an active part of the first generation of the five competencies, there should be an appreciation of resources necessary to sustain the cycle they establish as part of the operation. Employee teams should have been trained throughout the company on the customer experience development (CXD) process for improvement. The five competencies should now be embedded as part of building products, establishing services, and conducting annual planning.

Mature

You are now actively engaged in experience innovation and differentiation. By this phase, you should have tackled the majority of the irregular and unreliable customer experiences plaguing the customer journey along key touchpoints. This opens up resources for identifying and improving touchpoints for experience differentiation and innovation. By now, the use of your customer room to drive one-company focus and investments should have evolved to include leadership and all levels of the organization participation in stepping through the lives of your customers. Use the embedded competencies at this point to commit to differentiating moments in the customer journey. Employees should be able to work top down and bottom up, practicing the five competencies, to build these experiences.

Elevate

At this stage you have achieved company differentiation. Your company and people are differentiated in the marketplace by how you conduct yourself in business. By now, the five leadership competencies have been embedded into your business engine and are part of the way people work, and are compensated and rewarded. Annual planning begins with an understanding of the growth or loss of your customer asset and the inflection points along your journey where opportunity exists. Experience reliability is managed, and leaders care about the process metrics that impact customer asset growth with as much rigor as they care about outcome metrics such as sales goals. You use your customer journey framework to guide how the company hires and enables employees.

The work of your organization has gone beyond fixing unreliable experiences to creating differentiated memories. Your business decisions consistently set you apart because they are grounded in improving customers and employees' lives. You grow organically and through word of mouth. As a result, you earn an elevated position in the marketplace.

Our Move to 2 Pizza Teams = Agile, Fast Improvements

Curtis Kopf
Vice President, Customer Innovation
Alaska Airlines

Curtis Kopf is Vice President, Customer Innovation, at Alaska Airlines. His team of over 100 members is charged with making Alaska the world's easiest airline to fly. Teams span key customer touchpoints, including e-commerce, digital marketing, distribution, airport experience, R&D, employee tools, customer insight, and mobile.

To keep up and stay ahead of the increasingly changing needs of our customers, we knew we had to fundamentally change how we operated, including our organization. To become more agile, we decided to organize our teams more like a start-up or technology business, even though we are a more traditional type of company. To do this we borrowed a practice from my work at Amazon: organizing our teams into 2-pizza teams; teams small enough so you could serve the entire team with 2 pizzas. I have over one hundred people working to make customer experience improvements, and in the last year we've moved everyone to these small teams, including changing the physical environment in which they work. We eliminated all the cubes and offices to create a faster, more agile and collaborative environment and work product.

In the old way of doing things, whether through website feedback or some touchpoint with the customer, it might have taken us a month to make a change based on customer feedback. These small teams can fix a pain point in a week or two … and it has fundamentally changed the way we work. For example, customers wanted to see where they were on the upgrade list on the mobile app. The team went off and did that work and a month later we had that feature out.

Transformation Milestones

	Commit	Unite & Build	Embed	Mature	Elevate
	Commit & Drive 5 Competencies	Reliability Improvement	Experience Reliability	Experience Differentiation	Company Differentiation
Behavior of Leaders	Personally Involved in First Generation of 5 Competencies. Ensure teams have time to participate.	Focus Company On Priority Reliability Experiences. Invest in improvement teams & competency development.	United Leadership Accountability by Customer Journey Stage. Formalization of resources to sustain 5 Competencies.	Customer Life Improvement – Customer Room evolving to Identify & Commit to Differentiating Moments in Customer Journey	Decision making, hiring and actions consistent throughout company through lens of customer asset growth and life improvement.
Behavior of Employees	Select Individuals Participate in Competency Teams: Building First Generation of 5 Competencies.	Engaged teams learn and participate in "CXD": "CXD" – Customer Experience Development for priority experiences.	Five Competencies part of business improvement engine: "CXD" Competency Consistently Practiced by Teams.	Employee teams work top down and bottoms up, practicing the five competencies to build differentiated customer experiences.	One-company consistency in customer experience decision making. Collaborative silos find it easy to practice "CXD".

Years 1 through 3

Years 3 through 5

Years 5+

The chart above depicts the evolution of leadership and employee behavior as you move across the maturity model. All of my clients want to know how they can market and explain what will get done in what time frame, and this is meant to support you in that explanation. You can use it to assess where your efforts-to-date have brought you in transforming your leaders and organization.

As noted in the chart above, years one through three are the foundation building years. By year four, working through the skills of the five competencies and collaborative activities will start to become more organic. As you move past year three, the company will begin to shift as behaviors and decision-making are embedded that start with the customer. Levers that ensure this behavior is sustainable and evolving are formal and part of the structure of the organization during years four through five.

As you assess where you are in the maturity of embedding the equivalent of the five competencies, moving your organization from "commit" to "unite," here are tactics to engage or re-engage your leadership and organization:

- **Establish focus on honoring and managing customers as assets.**

  This is an important step to earn the right to do this work. Achieving this can only occur when there is consensus on how to measure this growth or loss, and that leaders start to use the language in a united manner to shift from survey score focus to customer asset growth.

- **Build a foundation in each of the five competencies.**

  The first generation of your five-competency engine will drive, in a very tactical manner, focus on customer experiences that are blocking customers from getting the most out of their experience with you, hindering customer asset growth. The workout of these initial issues will be identified through the journey framework and customer listening path of Competencies one and two.

- **Align Leaders to Focus on a Few Critical Reliability Areas.**

Begin with Experience RELIABILITY

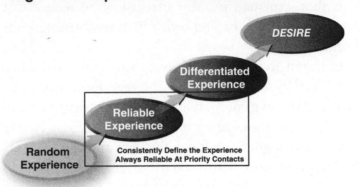

Aim leaders to focus on experience reliability and a few priorities. I can't tell you the number of companies who start with grandeur. Executives have been to a conference or read a book and they want to get to the wow moments. Don't fall into that trap. And don't boil the ocean by trying to improve the entire experience. Establishing a one-company framework for identifying and improving experiences is a new practice, so go slow and take on a focused few initially to learn. Then expand after learning is embedded. Otherwise, the weight of the work will cause it to cease to exist.

What you know already is that experience reliability is hard to achieve. The root cause of this lies firmly in the fact that there is no reliability in how to do this work. The selection and improvement approaches vary by silo and leader priority. So far, in most companies, a deeply rooted one-company approach to caring about and improving customer experiences and customer lives does not exist.

That is what these five competencies provide you: A way to embed a company-wide engine for experience reliability improvement. Over time, when evolved and improved, it will lead you to differentiation in your experiences, your decisions, and ultimately differentiate the type of company you show up as to customers and employees. In fact in many business models, increasingly this is the case: *experience reliability will differentiate you.*

- **Resist waiting to take action until everything is perfect.**

The resolution of the issues identified, first actions, and certainly your first customer room will feel clunky. I'm fine with clunky. I always tell my clients, "That just means you've begun!" Because these are competencies that will have impact only when they are built to be sustainable, make sure people know that they will evolve and constantly improve. Take a bite out of each of the competencies as soon as you can, but don't expect to do it all right away.

With these actions, clarity for the work and the role of the chief customer officer as the facilitator of the engine process will become clear. The process of building these initial actions with executives will give leaders the clearest understanding they have had regarding customer experience, what it is, and their active role required in the transformation.

We Began With How We Improve Customers' Lives

Sue Pregartner
Chief Operating Officer & Chief Customer Officer
Magisso North America, Inc.

Sue Pregartner is COO and Chief Customer Officer at Magisso North America, Inc., where she is responsible for the building and roll-out of the entire customer experience and operation of the North American market.

My job as the Chief Customer Officer is to bring our brand and brand experience of Finnish-based company Magisso to North America. This started with making sure that the entire leadership team and our board understands why we develop and deliver the products we do. And to make sure that the experience we deliver here connects with the North American customer.

(*continued*)

(*continued*)

When in discussion with the leadership team asking "define what Magisso does," for example, they described themselves as a "housewares" company. I have found it extremely important to educate our foreign leadership team that in the United States, the market needs to *feel* the brand. This means showing and engaging them in the nuances of the market. You can't assume that every market does the same thing. The boots on the ground in the market have to teach the leadership team what the needs are in the local market. We have to start with the customers' lives—their needs.

With my work, we have transformed that definition to "We design products to solve everyday problems that you have in your kitchen." We create objects that make your task easier. This contrasts greatly to how selling is done in Scandinavia, where products are described with features and not much emotion. Agreement on this customer and their needs was our first step toward building our operation for the United States.

We needed this important first step to begin to operationalize the business and the customer experience in the United States.

Evolving Organizational Structures

No head count? You're not alone. View this as a challenge and a test. As I mentioned in chapter two, often clarity has to be established to define the actions and outcomes of the role to earn the right to head count. You need to establish, with tactics, what the work will be to garner head count.

I am okay when a newly appointed chief customer officer is given a few months of runway to listen and understand, establish clarity, and start taking some early actions to earn the right to resources. I recommend using those first few months working with the leadership team (and a small extended team) to guide the build-out of your first version of the five competencies. This process establishes clarity for the leadership team in what a customer-driven transformation entails, uniting them in personally guiding the future direction, outcome, and timing of actions and culture change.

Engaging your Leadership Team in Version 1 of the Five Competencies

What is working quite well with my clients is building a team for each competency during the first four to six months. These teams thrive when C-suite leadership plays an active role in guiding the build-out of the "beta" versions of these competencies. We typically divide up the leadership team, assigning them by competency. The goal is to set a target date for the first customer room meeting in which the initial version of each competency team's work will be presented for the first time The chief customer officer supports and coordinates activities to keep everything moving toward executing the first customer room.

Here are the resources most customer leadership executives need within the first six months to frame the role and the work and get moving on actions. Sometimes these resources report to them, and in other situations they report elsewhere. We've seen initiating the role with success work in both of these instances.

1. Executive leadership team to engage in the build of the five competencies. This includes your CEO, CMO, CFO, CIO, etc.
2. Subject matter experts in organization to collaborate with and participate in the build of the five competencies.
   - Customer understanding—research, current segmentation, growth, and data
   - Communication
   - Change management
   - Culture—usually HR partners
   - High potential company members in operations, sales, product development, and IT

Earning the Right to Head Count

Earning the right to head count focused specifically on customer-driven transformation is achieved when you can show specific

CCO Team Resources by Year

	Commit	Unite & Build	Embed
	Commit & Drive 5 Competencies	Reliability Improvement	Experience Reliability
Engaged Company Participants	Leadership Commitment to Co-Lead First Generation Building of Five Competencies Company members tapped to participate on competency teams	Continued Leadership Engagement Cross-functional teams established per experience improvement priority	Continued Leadership Engagement Cross-functional teams established per experience improvement priority
Formal Organization	Chief Customer Officer 1-2 headcount assigned (temporarily) to first generation build full time.	Chief Customer Officer 1-3 headcount to formalize build out of 5 competency framework. Contractor headcount to facilitate CXD work teams.	Chief Customer Officer 2-8 headcount to embed & sustain 5 competencies. 2-6 headcount to facilitate cxd work teams.

Role Initiation through Year 1

Year 1 through Year 2

Year 3+

actions and prove value for the business and organization. Simply stated, headcount is powered by results and the ability to communicate and engage leaders in seeing value in the work. When the leadership team takes part in building the first generation of the five competencies (albeit a clunky version of the them), they appreciate the scale and scope of the work. And this workout provides clarity in appreciating and committing to permanent headcount and resources to continue building and sustain the five competencies customer-growth engine. The chart above represents a conservative staging of CCO team resources by year, based on initiating, building, embedding, and sustaining the five-competencies growth engine.

Once your first version of the five competencies engine is completed, the role of the chief customer officer and need for a team will be very clear. At this point, the decisions to be made are:

1. Skills and head count necessary to formalize the build-out of the five competency framework so it can be completed and repeated and refreshed every month, quarterly, and with annual planning.
2. The decision will need to be made in year one regarding customer experience facilitators to guide customer experience improvement teams in solving emerging customer issues.
3. New experience improvement teams will be assembled as leaders identify issues and opportunities to be addressed through the recurring customer room process, causing a constant need for these resources. Many of my clients hire skilled customer experience facilitators as contractors initially while they are learning the competency. Then after they've been through several improvement cycles they then decide whether to hire people into these roles permanently or continue to contract.

4. Over time your resource needs will grow, as more ongoing experience projects will be initiated on an ongoing basis with the cadence of your customer room.

   - You will be facilitating quarterly customer journey and annual planning reviews.
   - The customer listening path inputs will increase.
   - Your customer room audience may expand worldwide across multiple locations.

The key to headcount additions and what makes them successful is keeping leaders personally active, and as beneficiaries of what the five competencies deliver. By repeating the cycle of the customer room to drive accountability, and one-company decision-making, leaders will have increased clarity and value for the role and team. Head count to continue to provide these deliverables to the organization becomes easier to have approved when it is clear what the benefit is to stakeholders, their teams, and the company.

The Evolving Chief Customer Officer Role

The chief customer officer (CCO) role will evolve as you progress in implementing the five competencies, through the phases of the Customer Experience Maturity Map. Years one through three are what I call the "disruption and blocking and tackling years." Embedding competencies into the organization to focus and work together will disrupt deeply rooted silo-based operations and leadership.

People know how to achieve results within their silo walls. The CCO role and direction to move the organization in unison to improve customers' lives and earn customer-driven growth will disrupt definitions and metrics for success, work implementation, and organizational habits.

Successful chief customer officers deliberately build a plan of action in these early years to include uniting leadership actions and behavior, advancing from silo-based to one-company focus, embedding actions or competencies to achieve greater results, and enabling employee performance. "Early years" can mean the span of years one through three, depending on the size and complexity of the organization and ability to effect change.

Years 1 through 3: Chief Customer Officer Priorities	
UNITE	Unite leader actions, decisions, and behavior for customer-driven growth.
CONVINCE	Convince the organization, through listening and engaging them, that one-company focus will improve their results.
BUILD	Build and embed actions and competencies to achieve greater results.
FIX	Fix unreliable priority customer experiences. Remove employee obstacles.
PROVE	Prove the connection to customer and employee advocacy and growth. Deliver value. Earn the right to continue the work.

Year 4 and Beyond: Chief Customer Officer Priorities	
UNITE	Unite the organization to deliver differentiated experiences that elevate the role you play in customers' lives.
ENABLE	Enable maturity of decisions to improve customers' lives. Embed competencies to become the work of the organization.
PROVE	Prove the connection to customer and employee advocacy and growth. Deliver value. Earn the right to continue the work.

How I Stage My Work in This Role

Ingrid Lindberg
Chief Customer Experience Officer, Prime Therapeutics
Previously, Chief Customer Experience Officer, Cigna

Ingrid Lindberg is Chief Customer Experience officer for Prime Therapeutics. She was previously Cigna's Customer Experience Officer. Ingrid is responsible for design and implementation of Prime's customer experience strategy, which includes all interactions Prime has with its more than 25 million members, supporting them to get the medicine they need to feel better and live well.

Here's a high-level overview of key things I want to accomplish in my first three years in a customer experience role:

My first year is spent listening, planning and strategizing. I focus in year one on getting everyone on board, engaging both those who believe and those who don't. I also work to align the Future State Map into the organization's portfolio planning to determine an investment level for customer experience. As part of solving that equation, we will have begun the work on customer lifetime value so we have data and an algorithm that allows us to focus and invest in the work.

If I have done my job right in the first year, I will have also straightened out the math to be able to identify the top five big boulders that will give us the largest impact and the return on investment they will deliver. We then have the ammunition to support leaders in projects to get rid of the top three to five big boulders that make it hard for a customer to do business with us. We use the existing processes within the company for managing projects so that these don't appear to be layered on—but part of the regular business activities. I use the traditional method within the company to track performance on these efforts so they get monitored and managed just like a new product launch or a website build.

By year 2 I've changed compensation so it aligns to our customer experience metrics. A portion of compensation is dependent on our meeting those metrics. So when people ask me, "How do you get people to want to help you?" the answer is simple and clear. If compensation is set up right, everyone wants to participate.

After two to three years of doing this work and proving the regularity of how we solve problems and how they contribute a return, we ask for 30 percent of the portfolio investment to be dedicated to customer-experience-focused activities, and we make sure that anything else in the portfolio is doing no harm to our customers.

Summary

The five competencies of your customer-driven growth engine mature and improve as they have time to be embedded into how the company operates. Over time, the five competencies will move from being disruptive to part of business as usual. In this evolution, leadership and company member behavior will mature from requiring facilitation to collaborate to natural skill sets that are relied upon and embedded regularly throughout the organization.

The role of the CCO will evolves with this path, moving the organization to embedding competencies to earn the right to customer-driven growth. In phase one, often occurring from years one through three, activities are focused on uniting leadership and the organization, convincing people to participate, building the foundation for competencies, and fixing things to show proof and value. As the work matures and progresses, the CCO and his or her team unite the organization, but for purposes of elevated experience development and enabling the maturity of decisions and behavior that improve customers' lives.

When they are planned as a series of competencies to be embedded in how the business operates over time, they will progress to move your leaders and organization in the five customer experience maturity phases.

1. Commit
2. Unite and Build
3. Embed
4. Mature
5. Elevate

What all of us who have been Chief Customer Officers know is that the need for proving value for the role is omnipresent. It's that healthy dose of never feeling that we've done enough that forms the backbone of nearly every CCO I know and work with. It certainly was my ever-present companion when I held the role.

We need to prove it. The need to prove value is at the cornerstone of this work. **We must earn the right to continue to do the work.**

Establishing and Filling the Chief Customer Officer Role

Assembled here are resources to assist executives and candidates prepare your organization as you consider establishing a customer leadership executive role (Chief Customer Officer, Vice President of Customer Experience, etc.) role. I also invite recruiters whose phone calls I have welcomed with increasing frequency over the years to use these resources to frame this important role for their clients. These resources are framed into three sections.

The first section offers resources for assessing **organizational readiness** for the role. Two sets of research/audit questions are included. One is designed for executives to determine their need for a CCO, and one is questions for candidates to ask as they interview to assess commitment to the role. As a bonus, two chief customer officers, Martin Hand and Tish Whitcraft, who have both held this role multiple times, describe how they prepare to interview for this role.

The second section addresses **leadership engagement**. These provide you with leadership advocacy and engagement "conditions for success" important to the CCO role. Candidates and recruiters should know the state of these conditions as the role is developed. Candidates should probe to be aware of them as they are considering the role.

The third section focuses on **role definition**. Here you will find the successful attributes to look for in a CCO candidate. We use these extensively as I coach clients, and I can predict pretty accurately what their success will be based on my observations and understanding of these attributes. A new job description is included in this section, lined up with the five competencies. At my blog at www.customerbliss.com we will also be adding job descriptions of many customer leadership executives currently in the role who are graciously providing them for posting on the site. Here is a summary of all the resources in this chapter:

1. Organizational Readiness for the Role
   a. Interview Questions CCO Candidates Should Ask
   b. Do You Need a CCO?
   c. My Rock, My Story: "What I Needed Answered to Take This Role," by Martin Hand, Chief Donor/Customer Officer, St. Jude Children's Research Hospital
   d. My Rock, My Story: "How I Interview for Customer Leadership Roles," by Tish Whitcraft, Chief Customer Officer, OpenX
2. Leadership Engagement
   a. Eight CEO Actions to Increase CCO Success
   b. Are You Prepared to Bring a CCO into the C-suite?
   c. Will Your Power Core Enable or Inhibit the Work?
3. Role Definition
   a. Attributes of Successful Customer Leadership Executives
   b. Chief Customer Officer Job Description
   c. Current Job Descriptions of CCOs—at www.customer bliss.com

Readiness for the Role: Interview Questions CCO Candidates Should Ask

As you are considering taking on the role, or interviewing with an organization that wants to fill the CCO role, here are the high-level questions you must get answered. The answers you get will give you a sense if you will get the backing and commitment you need to make it a success.

1. Why This Work Now?

   Why the customer commitment now? What has changed? Is the company in a place to take on this work? Are there any impending issues to overshadow your ability to focus on this work?

2. Will You Elevate Customers as the Asset of Your Business?

   Moving focus to managing customers as assets requires a new view in how leaders define success for the organization and in how they demand accountability to include strategic customer metrics.

3. Will You Drive One-Company Experience Reliability?

   Customer-driven growth requires a one-company approach to improving priority customer experiences. Will you be able to question processes that worked for individual silos but don't work collectively for one-company customer driven growth?

4. Will You Develop the New Skills Required?

   Are you open to re-evaluating the skill sets for people and positions? Are you prepared to reinforce the need for building one-company, cross-functional solutions for customer experiences? This means process and change management and communication skills.

5. Is There a Commitment to Time and Resources?

   In the beginning, this is going to feel very much like new work layered onto existing work. Are you willing to commit resources from every part of the organization to participate in this work?

6. Does the CEO Sign Up to Be a True Partner?

Is this a key focus for you in decisions and actions? For example, if one of your best performers won't participate in or support this work, what will you do? Will you hold people accountable when people push back and question the importance of this work?

7. Is the C-Suite in Alignment?

Who are the advocates and who are the outliers and why?

8. Will You Insist on Corporate Patience?

Will you help everyone survive through the chaos of the shift to "the new normal"? This means managing board expectations and redefinitions of success. It takes discipline not to back down when the pressure to move faster or revert to cost management sets in—and it will.

Readiness for the Role: Do You Need a Chief Customer Officer?

Here is a very tactical set of questions, which is meant to accomplish two things for you. First, the explicit questions give you a platform to define the scope of work and specific work that a Customer Leadership Executive would take on. This takes the mystery out of the role. Second, if many of the responses to these questions are "no," it also provides you with a mandate to advance the exploration of the role.

1. There is someone in our company who clarifies what we are to accomplish with customers.

   ☐ Yes, there is

   ☐ No, there is not

   Implementation tip: These agreements need to be established in partnership with the functional owners across the organization. It is important to make sure that the CCO or executive leadership does not do this in a vacuum and then try to "throw the brick over the wall" to the leaders to rubber-stamp.

2. There is a clear process to drive alignment for what will be accomplished.

   ☐ Yes, there is

   ☐ No, there is not

   Implementation tip: Alignment is tricky. The best leaders I've worked with drive people into discussion by going around the table and asking each to state his or her commitment or dissent. These leaders make it okay to disagree if someone is not comfortable with what's being proposed. Think of alignment as requiring three steps: propose, put the idea out there for what will be accomplished, and don't suppose. Seek out dissenters and their reasons. Work out the solution and alternatives, and then ask for consensus again.

3. We have a road map for the customer work and know where progress will be measured.

   ☐ Yes, there is

   ☐ No, there is not

   Implementation tip: This needs to be a group effort. Bring together a team of people with at least one person from every operational area. This group needs to get into the ramifications and work involved in getting the priorities done.

4. Clear metrics exist for measuring progress that everyone agrees to use.

   ☐ Yes, there is

   ☐ No, there is not

   Implementation tip: Start with customer-asset metrics. Remember that simple is good and repetition works. Start here. Get everyone counting customer metrics consistently throughout the organization.

5. There is real clarity of everyone's roles and responsibilities.

   ☐ Yes, there is

   ☐ No, there is not

   Implementation tip: This is about the hand-offs between the silos. Make sure that there is clarity for which parts of the organization must come together to get the priorities accomplished. Too often these goals are kept lofty and high, and people aren't made accountable for their completion.

6. People really participate and care about the customer work.

   ☐ Yes, there is

   ☐ No, there is not

   Implementation tip: To make participation stick requires the commitment of the senior leadership to whom these people report and to create a partnership with them. Make participation in the customer work a privilege. Practice capacity management.

7. Appropriate resources are allocated to make a real difference to customers.

☐ Yes, there is

☐ No, there is not

Implementation tip: Hand waving without investment won't get you anywhere. The key here is to have an organized annual planning approach that dedicates time to the customer objectives and customer investment. The chief executive needs to be personally involved. To achieve success, specific actions with defined parameters of what needs to be accomplished must be identified. Investments that drive partial improvements in each area but don't connect in a real and meaningful way at the customer contact point have limited return on investment.

8. There is an understandable process for people to work together.

☐ Yes, there is

☐ No, there is not

Implementation tip: This work is as clear as mud. It starts with a high-level frenzy that in the blink of an eye has people going back to business as usual. The process for how the work will be defined, reviewed, executed, and rewarded has got to be laid out clearly.

9. The work is considered attainable.

☐ Yes, there is

☐ No, there is not

Implementation tip: There's a term that people used a lot at Microsoft: *boiling the ocean*. What I learned is to not abandon strategy but to dole it out in bite-size pieces. You need to know the end game. But then you need to bridge the gap between strategy and execution so people can work it into budgets, priorities, and planning.

10. A process exists for marketing achievements to customers and internally.

    ☐ Yes, there is

    ☐ No, there is not

    Implementation tip: What I've come to refer to as "marketing back" is often overlooked. When you don't tell people internally what's going on with the customer, it's all white noise to them. No report equals no action. You must make a point of marketing back to both your customers and internally inside the organization. I call this "marketing hope."

11. Recognition and reward are wired to motivate customer work.

    ☐ Yes, there is

    ☐ No, there is not

    Implementation tip: The customer work is not going to seem important until people start to be publicly commended and rewarded for it. Make every company gathering an opportunity to call out customer achievements and reward people for them.

Don't just ask these questions, *stew over them*. Debate them with your leadership and board. Is it realistic in your organization to divide and conquer these tasks without a customer leadership executive uniting them? If you can, your organization is well adjusted. It's the pushing and prodding part of the work that most companies need someone to spearhead. That becomes the role of the CCO.

If you decide to proceed with a CCO exploration, **make sure that you have consensus to proceed with the role**. The people whose sandbox the CCO will be in frequently had better agree up front to the company and to the discomfort that's to come as a result of the work. Think hard about your appetite and aptitude for the work. Temper this with the fact that this is at minimum a five-year journey. Pace yourself.

Readiness for the Role: My Rock, My Story

What I Needed Answered To Take This Position

Martin Hand
Chief Donor/Customer Officer
St. Jude Children's Research Hospital

Martin Hand is Chief Donor/Customer officer at St. Jude Children's Research Hospital, where he is responsible for the overall donor experience, contact center operations, and donor account processing functions. Martin was previously senior vice president of customer experience at United Continental Holdings.

Here's what I needed to be sure of before I took the role of first Chief Customer Officer in a non-profit organization. Establishing role clarity starts from the top down. The CEO needs to buy in and build buy-in across the organization. We need to focus on the customer/donor. We need to establish this work as strong and as understood a discipline as marketing, or operations, or any other business discipline. And this role has to report at the same senior level as the leaders of those disciplines.

When I was interviewing for this role, these were the things I needed to hear that made me believe this was a substantial role that could be successful:

1. Hearing that the focus in establishing this role was to make this work a core competency.
2. Being convinced that focusing on the building of this competency is understood to be a long-term view versus a short to medium view.
3. That the role has a seat at the table with the other chief officers of the company.
4. That the enterprise is bought into aligning around the donor— focusing on the donor and the donor experience.
5. That peers at the executive level were bought into this role and this work.

How I Interview for a Chief Customer Officer Role

Tish Whitcraft
Chief Customer Officer
OpenX

Tish Whitcraft is Chief Customer Officer at OpenX, responsible for the partner experience and all revenue growth and retention. OpenX is a global leader in web and mobile advertising technology that optimizes the economic potential of digital media companies through advertising technology.

In my experience, when companies are looking to fill a role like chief customer officer, it's often because something's broken. When I interview, I want to make sure the role is created for something more long-standing and strategic than just fixing holes and filling gaps.

When I talk to companies, my goal is to separate their short-term needs for the role. I can get the answer pretty quickly by asking these three questions: (1) where is the business going, (2) what does the company consider to be their competitive advantages, and (3) what do they consider a good investment in customer experience to be based on their company size? Finally, do they see this role as one with the autonomy to create new ways of doing business?

In tech businesses, there is an incredible connection between this role and informing what should be built into the product. This role has an influence over what is built and what it looks like. That is important—I want to be able to influence the product in addition to the user experience with the product. As I interview, my message is consistent: "I have to have influence and a vote in what you are building" for me to take on this role in a tech business. To me, that is just as important as understanding the CEO vision for the role. I will not come into a role at a CCO level without having a proper level of influence over the product development process—because that is half of the equation. To me, if it does not have that, it's not a CCO role—it's a VP of operations.

Leadership Engagement: Eight CEO Actions to Increase CCO Success

Senior executives should know *before* they decide on a CCO, that this position requires a personal commitment from them. There are eight major actions the CEO should do to ensure CCO success. These are written as notes to the CEO considering the role ...

1. **Take Personal Ownership**

   When the company commits to a CCO, the CEO should position the work as a priority of their agenda. Don't make it the sole mission of the CCO. People must understand that they will be delivering directly to you through working with the CCO.

   Commitment Questions:

   - Does your CEO clearly articulate what he/she wants the company to become for customers and constantly reinforce and drive the company in that direction?
   - Is there a commitment for organizational transformation, not some one-off tactics and silver bullets?

2. **Make the Customer Leadership Executive an Officer of the Company**

   It's illogical to think that your leaders will want to collaborate on strategy with a CCO who is not considered a peer. Ensure that the CCO has a role in the critical planning meetings to guarantee that the customer agenda is wired in. Incorporate part of your staff meetings to be facilitated by the CCO to drive the agenda. Especially in the early stages, make suggestions for meetings and events that the CCO should present at, participate in, or be invited to. I can't stress this point enough: If the CCO is not an officer, the customer effort will be greatly compromised. It's just plain human nature that peers won't be as anxious to be led by someone at a lower level. Don't put changing the course of human nature on the back of the CCO. The CCO will have enough to handle in working with you to change the course of how the company thinks about customers.

Commitment Questions:

- Has the CEO layered this work onto someone's already over-full plate, or is there recognition that this is a critical job for the organization that requires an immense time commitment?
- Has the CEO ensured that the role is positioned as an officer of the company with the full support and engagement of the CEO, leaders and the organization?

3. **Establish Acceptance/Role Clarity/Suspend Cynicism**

After initiating the CCO job, it's important to establish the working relationship between the company leadership and the CCO. Agree with the other leaders how they will personally engage with the CCO and how their organizations will participate with you.

Commitment Questions:

- Is the leadership team in alignment about the role and how they interact as a team?
- Is there clarity across the organization that this role is to enable and establish a one-company approach and discipline to customer experience, not to take over their work?

4. **Accelerate CCO Value Right Away**

Put the CCO in the position of doing specific and tangible work within the first month of the job. Engage the leadership team to be personally involved in guiding version one of the five competencies.

Make it the first order of business to drive the metrics of customer loyalty and customer profitability. Define your company's customer asset components, the players necessary to build them, and how leaders will work with the CCO to incorporate the metrics into the running of the business. If done well, this will further remove people's questions about the validity for the CCO and will move the company early on from talk to action. This type of tangible kick-start will help you gain the momentum you need for the long-term success of the CCO.

Commitment Questions:

• Are tactical projects put in motion so that people understand the role and its value?

• Are early-adapters and enthusiast leaders identified to work with first to prove role value?

5. **Drive Regular Accountability**

Demand regular accountability sessions for the sole purpose of identifying and tracking progress with the customer agenda. Don't make your CCO expend energy and cycles lobbying to get a place on the corporate agenda. That's the irony in this work that I've never quite understood. Why bring someone into the job and then make it nearly impossible that he or she be heard? Instead, establish a set of meetings with the specific agenda of discussing and advancing the customer experience work. Create continued clarity by having the CCO drive these meetings and steer the process. The CCO can create a flow and meeting focus by topic area and can facilitate the meetings. However, the executive sponsor will need to step in as the person asking for and expecting the performance.

Commitment Questions:

• Does your CEO actively hold people accountable for customer performance? Is there clarity in what's expected and does the organization practice discipline around identifying what should be measured and managed?

• Are forums for accountability regularly scheduled and enforced as a key strategic meeting for the success of the company?

6. **Provide Political Air Cover**

What the CCO needs most is someone at the highest levels to collaborate with, who is willing to step in and course-correct the action when it stalls. And it will stall. A CCO who is forced to navigate this work alone will wear out over time as the isolation of the job mounts. An absent executive sponsor who is there just to sign checks and attend the pitch meetings isn't going to have the level of understanding to be able to advance or rate the work. It takes such a strong internal push for people in these positions to stay singularly focused on this work. Motivate the motivator by providing the air cover that he or she must have to get the job done.

Commitment Questions:

- Does your CEO commit time and resources to be a solid partnership with the customer leader?
- Does your CEO play an active role in understanding and participating in the rigor of aligning the company when necessary?

7. **Insist on Corporate Patience**

The customer experience work is not for the mild-mannered or for the quarterly inclined. People are going to need to understand that this is a multiyear endeavor. They can't bail in the first year. That would be a huge waste of human and financial capital. It will be the executive sponsor's job to get everyone to stay the course. The CEO must set realistic expectations that this is at minimum a three- to five-year path.

Commitment Questions:

- Is your CEO committed to the timeline required (in the neighborhood of five years) and are they willing to suspend the usual short-term expectations of immediate results and have the patience for the customer work to take hold and yield results?

- Will they sustain the patience inside the corporation and with the board to stay the course so that results can be achieved?

8. **Demystify the Road Map**

To create the shift for an organization to cohesively deliver customer experiences is a huge undertaking. Yet it's quickly agreed to when that charge comes from the president: *"We must improve customer relationships and profitability."* Who wouldn't salute that flag? But what flag did the company salute? What did they agree to accomplish? Therein lies the problem: the CEO's request for customer commitment contains no direction.

The organization doesn't know what they've agreed to do or how they'll get it done. The CCO can provide significant value to the CEO and company leadership by framing the scale of the undertaking and establishing a road map for getting the work accomplished over time.

Commitment Questions:

- Are expectations and processes to drive the work identified realistically and planned so that people understand the road map, where it is leading and why it is set forth?
- Have the resources been applied so that the road map is grounded in the reality of what the company can achieve and fund?

Leadership Engagement: Are You Prepared to Bring a CCO into the C-Suite?

Bringing a CCO into the C-suite will change the dynamic of that group. The CCO role, unlike others sitting around that table, will not necessarily "own" an operation. Instead the CCO will engage as an influencer of the priorities of the organization, culture and the competencies required to enable customer-driven growth. Therefore the leadership team must be committed and ready for this new role to have a seat at their table. The two big topics to make sure you get out in the open and discuss are listed below.

1. **C-Suite Agreement on the Role**

   - Is everyone in agreement on the need for a CCO at this time?
   - Is there agreement on the purpose and actions of your CCO?
   - Will you advance a respected leader from within the organization who has run a successful customer-driven organization to the CCO role, or will you hire from outside?
   - Will all C-suite members be involved in the hiring and selection of the CCO?
   - Has the board committed to the role and the reason for the role?
   - Is there agreement that this is a commitment for a minimum of five years?

2. **C-Suite Working Relationship with the CCO**

   - Have you worked through that the CCO will challenge current ways of solving problems and identifying priorities, to focus us on driving customer-driven growth? Is everyone okay with that?
   - Does everyone agree that cultural work will need to be done as part of this work? This is not just about projects

and work streams, but a transformation of how you will and will not grow?

- Does the C-suite agree to actively participate in the work with the CCO? For example, will they champion the beta version of the five competencies?
- Is there agreement that it will be necessary as part of this work to unite in prioritization of investments and commitments?
- Is everyone comfortable that building out a one-company approach will challenge the metrics and processes that they currently "own"?
- Is there agreement to build one-company teams to establish customer-driven solutions?

Leadership Engagement: Will Your Power Core Enable or Inhibit the Work?

Assess Your Power Core Impact on Moving Forward

As you consider a Chief Customer Officer for your organization, understanding your company's power core is an important step in determining the challenges ahead in your transformation, and the ease with which you can proceed with a CCO role. These are some quick tools to assess how the agenda and priorities set by the power core are in sync with the five customer-leadership competencies.

Use the tools below to identify your power core and the set of kick-start actions that will engage your power core leaders in this work. Evaluate if they are prepared and committed to take on the work identified. Companies typically forge ahead with the customer work without taking stock of these very real and powerful determinants of its success. They simply begin, hit the inevitable roadblocks of the power core, and from there the work begins to falter and sputter.

Action 1: Identify Your Company Power Core

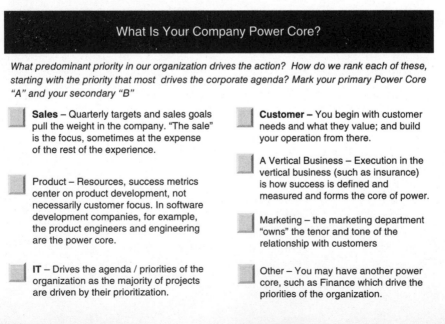

What Is Your Company Power Core?

What predominant priority in our organization drives the action? How do we rank each of these, starting with the priority that most drives the corporate agenda? Mark your primary Power Core "A" and your secondary "B"

Sales – Quarterly targets and sales goals pull the weight in the company. "The sale" is the focus, sometimes at the expense of the rest of the experience.

Product – Resources, success metrics center on product development, not necessarily customer focus. In software development companies, for example, the product engineers and engineering are the power core.

IT – Drives the agenda / priorities of the organization as the majority of projects are driven by their prioritization.

Customer – You begin with customer needs and what they value; and build your operation from there.

A Vertical Business – Execution in the vertical business (such as insurance) is how success is defined and measured and forms the core of power.

Marketing – the marketing department "owns" the tenor and tone of the relationship with customers

Other – You may have another power core, such as Finance which drive the priorities of the organization.

Action 2: Assess whether Leaders Will Engage in Kick-Start Actions

When Product Is Your Power Core

Product strength in the marketplace means that you are doing well at understanding your competition and are strong about determining where to focus. Sustaining that position of strength is dependent on staying relevant. There are clear product development metrics. However, the customer experience wrapped around that product may be lacking.

Kick-Start Actions for Integrating the Customer into the Product Power Core.

The company needs a strong senior advocate within product leadership to move this work forward in a product-driven organization. Sharing the customer leadership agenda with the product area is key. Forging a partnership with them and acknowledging the power they wield in driving the customer to the company is critical. Keep working on the approach. Don't develop solutions on your own and then try to get them to sanction it or bless it—it won't work.

- Focus on product development, based on customer priorities.
- Establish a product feedback loop directly to product development teams.
- Create initial performance standards grounded in high-value drivers.
- Institute tracking and reporting at the C-suite level.
- Introduce customer asset metrics.

When Sales Is Your Power Core

When the sales organization is the power core, the sales force is a well-oiled machine that knows how to target and close customers. However the connectivity between the sale and the overall customer experience can be your Achilles' heel.

For example: How do you ensure customers receive information to use and operate products post-sale? Is there a smooth transition as someone moves from prospect to customer? Does the sales team consider it their job to resell the company and products when subscriptions, services, and products are up for renewal? Are they rewarded as equally for both new customer acquisition and growth of existing customers?

Kick Start for Integrating the Customer into the Sales Power Core

- Commit to focus on net customer asset growth, not just acquisition.
- Establish a "defector pipeline" identifying where customers must have reliable one-company experiences to drive growth.
- Commit to no more than five areas on the defector pipeline.
- Reward sales performance in keeping and growing customers, not just acquisition.
- Introduce customer asset metrics.

When Information Technology (IT) or Engineering Is Your Power Core

When information technology (IT) is the power core, the ability to weave customer-driven growth into the organization is a bit of a wild card based on leadership, its ability to bring the silos together, and the organizational appetite for delivering a unified platform to customers.

When IT drives priorities, investments can often allocated by jobs, projects, and what can be executed by quarter. You have a clear idea of what you can expect to roll out each year. Metrics are specific to operational execution areas. With a strong IT power core, you could be fortunate to be far along on the continuum of collecting and using customer data and feedback. Strong IT departments push very hard for the business leaders to provide clear requirements for the application of resources. That means people must justify what they're doing to get funding.

Kick-Start for Integrating the Customer into the IT Power Core

The first job is making IT a true partner in the customer experience mission. People make the mistake of bringing IT in too late in the game. You've got to define the five-competencies as the work, and IT needs to be sitting at the table when this happens.

- Make information technology a partner in the customer mission.
- Identify the customer priorities.
- Create an oversight process for aligning IT resources with customer priorities.
- Recast IT priorities = customer priorities.
- Engage IT in the customer asset metrics.

When a Vertical Business Is Your Power Core

When a vertical business is your company's power core, you have deep competencies in an area of business, such as hospitality, or insurance, or accounting. And you have become known in the marketplace because of this competency. Your organization has a strong set of metrics to guide the operational execution, such as how to execute a claim with efficiency for your operation.

Companies with a strong basis in a vertical business can lose sight of the customer along the way. The thing they are best at becomes the definition of the business. Thinking can often be inside out, starting with what's important to the company's efficiency. In this type of environment, each of the silos tends to look at its part of the operation as separate and distinct. Execution is therefore separate and distinct.

Kick-Start for Integrating Customer Focus into the Vertical Business Power Core

A good first step: initiate a company-wide conversation to establish clarity of purpose. What and how will you improve customers' lives? Since this may or may not ever have been a discussion at an operational level, it's important to bring together those who run the business into these decisions. Many times "who we are" is a marketing branding exercise that doesn't cascade throughout the organization or is ignored with the hand wave: "That's marketing's work. We're running the business."

- Redefine your business to understand relevance to customers.
- Clarify what you want to deliver and why. Gain consensus.
- Map the experience and top 10 customer interactions for delivery.
- Begin to track and manage performance in the top ten interactions.
- Introduce Customer Asset Metrics.

When Marketing Is Your Power Core

When marketing is the power core, it's a bit of a wild card. Some marketing functions own the customer experience. In this case, they have taken on the comprehensive efforts companywide. They are working to connect the operating areas for delivery of the contact points, and they are connecting the messaging and data. That's an evolved environment. More traditionally, when the power core is marketing, the focus on the customer relationship is about marketing campaigns and tactics. Brand at the advertising messaging level is emphasized, but partnering with the operating areas for how to deliver the brand experience can fall short. The biggest part of the work here is not in convincing the marketing power core of the importance of the work but in gaining its acceptance of its scope and expansive responsibilities.

Kick-Start for Integrating the Customer into the Marketing Power Core

This work requires additional skill sets beyond traditional marketing campaigns, data management, and communication plans. It requires process work, change management, and new leadership approaches. It requires the development of different motivation and reward programs and a whole new approach to accountability.

- Gain agreement for the scope of work—beyond traditional marketing.
- Create process and change management competencies.
- Map customer experience and priority experiences.
- Improve priority experiences.
- Introduce customer asset metrics.

Customer Power Core

When customer-driven growth is the power core, decisions emanate from understanding what will drive the greatest value to customers in the short and long terms. The company's long-term desire is to deliver a differentiated customer experience to drive the greatest amount of profitable customers.

The customer power core is still rare, surprisingly, after all these years of effort. Businesses that are led with the customer as their power core are the companies known in the marketplace to be best for customers. These companies begin with the customer in their decision-making and operations.

In a company with a customer power core, customer needs drive the overall plan for what's developed and delivered.

As you are seeking candidates for the CCO role, or are seeking the role for yourself, this list of aptitudes will be most helpful. These are the common attributes possessed by successful customer leadership executives. Candidates will find this list helpful to determine if their skills and interests connect with the success factors for this role. Recruiters and executives seeking candidates both internally and externally can use these to observe and evaluate skill sets of potential CCOs.

10 Aptitudes:

Successful CCOs

1. Revenue = attention
2. Customer asset metrics
3. Make them listen
4. Persist!
5. Action, not crystal balls
6. Survival of the chameleon
7. Keep the troops positive
8. Market back
9. Create urgency
10. Give the power away

1. **Revenue = Attention**

   A customer leader has got to be able to make and prove this case to gain executive and board support. Customer leaders must attach this work to the profitability of the business.

2. **Customer Asset Metrics**

   A customer leader gets the customer on the agenda of every key meeting. Customers are discussed as humans, as people we either kept or drove away. Customer leaders make it painful to ignore the fact that our actions every day either grow or shrink the customer base.

3. **Make Them Listen**

   A customer leader translates the customer information into compelling, disruptive and engaging nuggets of information. They make people eager to know more.

4. **Persist!**

   How do we do with resistance? Do we thrive on it or just survive? We need to be comfortable persisting, even when we're turned down.

5. **Action, Not Banners and Coffee Mugs**

   The company will need to see substantive change to believe that the commitment is true and real and understand what it means in terms of things they should do. The customer leader's job is to keep it real. There have likely been efforts that have come before this most recent proclamation to the customer. The corporate memory keepers have little patience for empty commitment to the customer.

6. **Survival of the Chameleon**

   Customer leaders should understand the functions of the organization. Most important, customer leaders need to know the players and what their hot buttons are. Use this knowledge to thrive as a chameleon, modifying approaches as necessary to connect with each part of the organization.

7. **Keep the Troops Positive**

   Customer leaders know that their teams and all of the assembled teams working on experience improvement need reinforcement. They keep the troops positive by ensuring leadership participation, capacity creation and rewards. They highlight and recognize efforts and results.

8. **Market Back—Marketing Hope**

   In a customer leadership job, you must understand what customers and the company need, deliver it to them, and remind them that you gave it to them.

Marketing back helps customers believe that the company is listening and acting on their words. It jolts the naysayer out of thinking things can't or won't get done. It's absolutely essential to getting the future momentum you need by feeding the organization hope, one morsel at a time.

9. **Create Urgency**

Customer leaders clarify for the organization exactly which issues and experiences are keeping or repelling customers. They simplify the work, and with that simplicity, make it easier and more compelling for people to want to take action!

10. **Give the Power Away**

Astute customer leaders understand that this unique power they possess cannot be abused; in fact, it must be given away. With strong advocate partnerships, one of the greatest tools a customer leader has to continue motivating participation is having people present their own actions, and putting them front and center to take the credit.

Role Definition: New CCO Job Description

The Chief Customer Officer (or Customer Experience Executive) **works with the organization to earn the right to customer-driven growth.** This leader works with the board, the C-suite, and across the organization to embed behaviors and actions that unite silo-based organizations in focusing on priorities in customers' lives. This manner of doing business honors employees and customers, resulting in a sustainable, repeatable and deliberate one-company approach to growth.

The goals of the CCO include:
- Uniting the C-suite as leaders in the transformation.
- Establishing one-company definitions and goals for customer growth.
- Embedding competencies to improve and innovate experiences.
- Building a culture that begins with the lives of customers.
- Enabling employees to deliver value.

The actions of the CCO are to embed these competencies:
1. *Honoring and Managing Customers as Assets of the Business*
   - Enable and inspire decision-making driven by honoring customers as assets.
   - Elevate customer growth/loss as success metric of the business.
   - Build one-company definitions of customer segments, customers to invest in.
   - Establish behavioral indicators of growth or loss of relationship.
   - Unite leadership in customer-asset growth definition and communication.

2. *Aligning around Experience: Uniting the Organization to Deliver Valued Customer Experiences*

- Lead one-company prioritization of investment on high-impact experiences.
- Establish one-company journey maps and identification of priority experiences.
- Create a common language set and definitions for the customer experience.
- Unite the organization on the evaluation of experience reliability performance.
- Help leaders deliver united communication and focus on experiences.

3. *Build a Customer Listening Path: Establish Active Customer Listening and Understanding*

- Be the storyteller of customers' lives.
- Define what customers value and understand evolving needs
- Unite aided feedback, such as surveys to tell a one-company customer story.
- Unite unaided feedback, such as social media to tell a one-company customer story.
- Align multiple sources of customer feedback to the customer journey.
- Create a united platform for understanding customers' lives & focused action.

4. *Proactive Experience Reliability and Innovation*

- Embed skills to understand and improve priority experiences.
- Build a customer experience development process to enable cross-company teams to improve unreliable and innovation opportunity experiences.
- Teach teams to build reliability metrics for priority experiences.

- Elevate priority process metrics in critical experiences to earn C-suite focus.
- Manage priority experience processes proactively to earn customer growth.
- Identify and focus on customer behavior movement as a result of priority experiences to establish connection and ROI to customer-driven growth.

5. *One-Company Leadership, Accountability, and Decisions*

- Unite leaders in focusing the organization on improving customers' lives.
- Engage leaders personally in the build out of the competencies.
- Unite leadership communication and messaging.
- Enable employees to deliver value. Get rid of stupid rules and barriers.
- Establish experiential learning for walking in the customers' shoes.
- Drive rigorous communication and engagement.
- Unite leaders in building a lens for decision-making that begins with growing customers as assets.

Your Next Steps ...

My goal in writing this book was to establish clarity for what it takes to lead a customer-driven business transformation, and to establish value for the role of the chief customer officer. In defining the five competencies that build a customer-driven growth engine with the CCO as the architect, my goal was to translate the complex work of customer experience and cultural transformation into understandable, achievable actions. I wanted to provide insight into what comprises a customer-driven transformation, and show the benefits of having a dedicated chief customer officer work across your organization to embed these five proven competencies with your leadership team.

I hope that this content has been valuable to you, and that I have "earned the right to" become a trusted resource for you in your work to improve customers' lives. When you need help with your transformation, are considering a chief customer officer role, or would like to chat about this work, I hope you'll reach out.

You can find me at www.customerbliss.com, You'll find more resources on this content and my blog there. You can also connect with me on Twitter, @jeannebliss. It will be an honor to connect.

Acknowledgments

The role of the customer leadership executive, more than almost any other role, prospers by standing on the shoulders of those who came before us, to learn from their journeys. And from sharing fearlessly with those currently in the trenches about what works and what doesn't.

To that end, this is my "pay it forward" book to all the people whose shoulders I have stood on throughout my years in this business, learning and toiling away as a practitioner for over twenty years. This book is also my thank-you to my clients who have invited me to partner with them in their work since 2002. It is a privilege to do the work of improving customers' lives alongside you.

Finally, an enormous debt of thanks goes to the following customer leadership executives whose "My Rock, My Story" vignettes bring this book to life. What a pleasure it has been working with you! I look forward to continuing our conversations.

Graham Atkinson is Chief Marketing and Customer Experience Officer at **Walgreens**, the largest drug retailing chain in the United States. Graham has responsibility for the full customer experience/relationship, including loyalty.

Mike Bennett is Senior Vice President, Operations at the **Irvine Company Office Properties**, where he leads their customer-driven transformational effort with the leadership team that began in 2010 and continues today. Irvine Company Office Properties manages a portfolio of 500 office and industrial properties throughout California.

Samir Bitar is Director of the Office of Visitor Services at **Smithsonian Institution**, where he is responsible for developing overseeing the implementation of the inaugural visitor experience strategy, which addresses all visitor touch points across the Smithsonian's 19 museums, galleries, and national zoo.

Tom Botts is Executive Vice President and Chief Customer Officer at **Denihan Hospitality Group**, responsible for developing and executing a holistic approach to customer experience across brands and properties. Denihan Hospitality group is a full-service hotel management and development company that owns and/or operates boutique hotels in major urban markets in the United States.

Claire Burns is Chief Customer Officer at **MetLife**. She drives the customer-centric strategy and actions to build customer empathy and improve the experience of purchasing, maintaining, and enhancing customer coverage with MetLife. MetLife, Inc., is a global provider of insurance, annuities, and employee benefit programs.

Alison Circle is Chief Customer Experience Officer at **Columbus Metropolitan Library**, where she is responsible for the overall library experience and management of 23 libraries and more than 700 staff members. Columbus Metropolitan Library is one of the most-used library systems in the United States, and is consistently among the top-ranked public libraries.

Heather Carroll Cox is Chief Client Experience, Digital and Marketing Officer at **Citi,** where she is responsible for the vision, strategy, structure, and execution of a common client experience, driving global NPS copyright efforts and leading digital, marketing, and decision management across global consumer banking.

Jeb Dasteel is Senior Vice President, Chief Customer Officer at **Oracle,** where he is responsible for development and implementation of Oracle's strategy for maximizing the value of customers as a core company asset.

This includes driving organizational focus on the success of our customers and harnessing that success to drive incremental revenue for Oracle through customer feedback, analytics, care, response, communications, customer marketing, and advocacy programs.

Chris Dawson is Vice President & General Manager, Consumer Experience and Global Sales Division, for **BRP— Bombardier Recreational Products**. He leads global consumer experience, sales management, go-to market activities, network development, after-sales service, parts, accessories, and clothing for Ski-Doo, Lynx, Can-Am, and Sea-Doo brands, and Evinrude in international markets.

Susan DeLaney is Vice President, Customer Experience at **UPS** where she is responsible for ensuring UPS customer experience principles are understood, implemented, and upheld at all touch points, in all business units and geographies. United Parcel Service serves more than 220 countries and territories worldwide.

Scott Dille is Senior Vice President and Director of Client and Employee Experience at **Northern Trust**, where he leads research, design, and measurement of the client and employee experience. Northern Trust is a global leader delivering innovative wealth management, asset management, and asset servicing to corporations, institutions and affluent individual and families.

Gavan Duff is Chief Customer Officer for **MSA, The Safety Company**, where he leads their global strategy and implementation for customer experience transformation. MSA is the world's leading manufacturer of safety products designed to protect people throughout the world.

Nick Frunzi is Chief Customer Officer at **ESRI**, where he directs strategy, metrics, requirements, and resources to enhance customer retention and loyalty and create competitive advantage. ESRI is the world's largest geospatial technology provider, enabling governments, industry leaders and many other to connect with the analytic knowledge they need to make critical decisions that shape the planet.

Martin Hand is Chief Donor / Customer Officer at **St. Jude Children's Research Hospital,** where he is responsible for the overall donor experience, contact center operations, and donor account processing functions. Martin was previously Senior Vice President of Customer Experience at United Continental Holdings.

Aisling Hassell is Head of International Customer Experience at **Airbnb,** where she is responsible for the global customer experience. Airbnb is a community marketplace for people to list, discover, and book unique accommodations around the world in more than 34,000 cities and 190 countries.

Curtis Kopf is the Vice President, Customer Innovation at **Alaska Airlines.** His team of over 100 members is charged with making Alaska the world's easiest airline to fly. Teams span key customer touch points, including e-commerce, digital marketing, distribution, airport experience, R&D, employee tools, customer insight, and mobile.

Ingrid Lindberg is Chief Customer Experience Officer for **Prime Therapeutics**. She was previously **Cigna**'s Customer Experience Officer. Ingrid is responsible for design and implementation of Prime's customer experience strategy, which includes all interactions Prime has with its more than 25 million members, supporting them to get the medicine they need to feel better and live well.

Misha Logvinov is Chief Customer Officer at **Lithium Technologies**. Misha is responsible for leading Lithium's strategic programs to ensure long-term customer success and enhancing and solidifying Lithium's customer-centric culture by orchestrating the entire customer value chain across functions and geographies.

Lesley Mottla is Senior Vice President of Customer Experience at LAUNCH. Lesley was part of the management team that developed **Zipcar**'s award-winning customer experience and technologies. She just joined **LAUNCH**, a start-up devoted to reinventing multichannel consumer experiences.

Hilary Noon is Vice President of Marketplace Insight and Experience at **The American Cancer Society**. In her role she is the thought leader responsible for driving customer-focused strategy at the C-suite and business-unit owner levels of the organization.

Dan Pastoric is Executive Vice President and Chief Customer Officer at **Enersource Corporation** in Ontario, Canada, where he is leading corporate strategy, increasing shareholder value in both the regulated and nonregulated businesses. He manages all customer care service functions including conservation and demand management.

Mary Poppen is Chief Customer Officer at **SAP, Global Cloud Business**. She is responsible for the definition, measurement, and improvement of the total customer experience, including engagement, value and adoption, research, and operational transformation across SAP Cloud lines of business.

Sue Pregartner is COO and Chief Customer Officer at **Magisso North America, Inc.**, where she is responsible for the building and rollout of the entire customer experience and operation of the North American market. Magisso designs and distributes products globally to solve everyday problems you have in your kitchen.

Carol Pudnos is Head of Global Patient Experience at **AbbVie**, a global biopharmaceutical company. Her role is to bring the customer journey to life inside the enterprise, educating employees and transforming the culture, engaging all stakeholders to deliver excellent customer experiences.

She was previously Vice President of Customer Experience at **Dow Corning Corporation**.

Taylor Rhodes is President & CEO of **Rackspace**. He was previously Senior Vice President & Chief Customer Officer. Rackspace is a leader in managed cloud—delivering cloud-computing as a managed service for more than 300,000 businesses worldwide.

Mark Slatin is Senior Vice President, Client Experience Manager, at **Sandy Spring Bank**, where he leads the client experience effort as a key strategic initiative to drive sustainable growth across all business units. With $4.4 billion in assets, Sandy Spring Bank provides comprehensive financial solutions to clients across Maryland and Northern Virginia.

Kevin Thompson is Vice President of Customer Experience and Development at luxury retailer **Barneys New York**. Kevin is responsible for managing the highest service standards across all company touch points, including stores, restaurants, e-commerce, and credit services, to create a seamless omni-channel brand experience.

Lambert Walsh is Vice President and General Manager at **Adobe**, where he leads Adobe's efforts to retain and grow long-term relationships with customers and partners across all segments and lines of business. He has led customer success at Adobe since 2007.

Jeri Ward is Director, Customer Experience at **Audi of America, Inc.,** where she is the senior leader for customer experience strategy, insights, and transformation across the enterprise.

Brenda Wensil is Chief Customer Experience Officer at the **U.S. Department of Education—Federal Student Aid**. Brenda established the first-ever role in customer experience for the federal government. She is an executive leader in the U.S. Department of Education's Federal Student Aid; the largest single source of funding for postsecondary education in the United States, and a member of the organization's executive operating committee.

Tish Whitcraft is Chief Customer Officer at **OpenX**, responsible for the partner experience and all revenue growth and retention. OpenX is a global leader in web and mobile advertising technology that optimizes the economic potential of digital media companies through advertising technology.

Robert Wiltz is Chief Customer Officer at **Paris Presents, Inc.**, where his role is to transform the go-to market approach for the company, focusing on customer development and brand building. Paris Presents is a leading provider of branded and private label personal care products, distributing through national and global retailers.

Pete Winemiller is Senior Vice President of Guest Relations for the **NBA's Oklahoma City Thunder**. He is charged with creating repeat customers in a business environment where you cannot control the level of success on the basketball court, but you can control what happens in the stands.

Finally, a personal note of thanks to my husband, Bill Bliss. My life experience is exponentially improved because you are in it.

About the Author

A passionate customer experience practitioner, Jeanne Bliss pioneered the role of the chief customer officer, holding the role for over 20 years at Lands' End, Allstate, Microsoft, Coldwell Banker, and Mazda corporations. She now runs CustomerBliss, (www.customerbliss.com), a global customer experience transformation company with clients such as AAA, Brooks Brothers, St. Jude Children's Research Hospital, and Bombardier Aerospace. She is a global keynote speaker on these topics, and sought frequently by major media for her input and points of view. Jeanne is the co-founder of the Customer Experience Professionals Association, established to advance the worldwide discipline of customer experience and customer experience practitioners. Her two best-selling books are *Chief Customer Officer: Getting Past Lip Service to Passionate Action*, and *I Love You More than My Dog: Five Decisions that Drive Extreme Customer Loyalty in Good Times and Bad*. She lives in Los Angeles with her husband, Bill.

Index